Why Democracies Need
an Unlovable Press

For Margie

Why Democracies Need an Unlovable Press

Michael Schudson

polity

This collection first published in 2008 by Polity Press
Reprinted 2009

Polity Press
65 Bridge Street
Cambridge CB2 1UR, UK

Polity Press
350 Main Street
Malden, MA 02148, USA

ISBN-13: 978-0-7456-4452-3
ISBN-13: 978-0-7456-4453-0 (paperback)

A catalogue record for this book is available from the British Library.

Typeset in 10.5 on 12 pt Times
by SNP Best-set Typesetter Ltd., Hong Kong
Printed and bound in Great Britain by the MPG Books Group

The publisher has used its best endeavours to ensure that the URLs for external
websites referred to in this book are correct and active at the time of going to
press. However, the publisher has no responsibility for the websites and can
make no guarantee that a site will remain live or that the content is or will
remain appropriate.

For further information on Polity, visit our website: www.polity.co.uk.

Contents

Acknowledgements

The author and publisher gratefully acknowledge the permission granted to reproduce the copyright material in this book.

Chapter 3 originally appeared as "The US Model of Journalism: Exception or Exemplar?" in Hugo de Burgh, ed., *Making Journalists: Diverse Models, Global Issues* (Abingdon: Routledge, 2005). Reproduced with permission of the publisher.

Chapter 5 originally appeared as "Why Democracies Need an Unlovable Press" in Timothy E. Cook, ed., *Freeing the Press: The First Amendment in Action* (Baton Rouge: Louisiana State University Press, 2005). Reproduced with permission of the publisher.

Chapter 6 originally appeared as "The Concept of Politics in Contemporary U.S. Journalism," *Political Communication* 24/2 (2007) pp. 131–42.

Chapter 7 originally appeared as "What's Unusual about Covering Politics as Usual" in Barbie Zelizer and Stuart Allan, eds., *Journalism After September 11* (London and New York: Routledge, 2002). Reproduced with permission of the publisher.

Chapter 8 originally appeared as "The Anarchy of Events and the Anxiety of Story Telling," *Political Communication* 24/3 (2007) pp. 253–7.

Chapter 9 originally appeared as "Why Conversation is not the Soul of Democracy," *Critical Studies in Mass Communication* 14/4 (1997) pp. 297–309. Reproduced with permission of the publisher (www. informaworld.com).

Chapter 10 originally appeared as "The Trouble with Experts – and Why Democracies Need Them," *Theory and Society* 35 (2006) pp. 491–506. With kind permission of Springer Science and Business Media.

1

Introduction: facts and democracy

In the late 1960s, political philosopher Hannah Arendt observed that truth and politics "are on rather bad terms with each other." She saw that power threatened truth, particularly "factual truth." Formal truths like "two plus two equals four" are not as vulnerable as factual truth because "facts and events – the invariable outcome of men living and acting together – constitute the very text of the political realm."[1] Not incidentally, they also constitute the text of journalism.

Arendt wrote in defense of facts, but this was not easy. Even in the 1960s, the concept of a fact was under indictment. "Do facts," Arendt asked,

> independent of opinion and interpretation, exist at all? Have not generations of historians and philosophers of history demonstrated the impossibility of ascertaining facts without interpretation, since they must first be picked out of a chaos of sheer happenings (and the principles of choice are surely not factual data) and then be fitted into a story that can be told only in a certain perspective, which has nothing to do with the original occurrence?

Arendt concedes all this but then boldly asserts that these perplexities "are no argument against the existence of factual matter, nor can they serve as a justification for blurring the dividing lines between fact, opinion, and interpretation, or as an excuse for the historian to manipulate facts as he pleases."[2]

Arendt tells a story of Georges Clemenceau, prime minister of France during World War I, who, a few years after the war, was discussing the question of who was responsible for initiating the horrendous bloodshed of that conflict Clemenceau was asked what future historians would say. He replied, "This I don't know. But I know for certain that they will not say Belgium invaded Germany." Arendt then adds that this is not just up to the historians, that it would take "a power monopoly over the entire civilized world" to erase the fact that, on August 4, 1914, German troops crossed into Belgium rather than Belgian troops crossing into Germany. And then – ever a realist – she adds that "such a power monopoly is far from being inconceivable, and it is not difficult to imagine what the fate of factual truth would be if power interests, national or social, had the last say in these matters."[3]

Is there any way out of this battle between politics and truth? For Arendt, it depends on how politics operates in a particular instance. Some political systems tolerate or even encourage the establishment of institutions that stand at arm's length from power. She cites the judiciary and the academy as two domains where "at least in constitutionally ruled countries, the political realm has recognized, even in the event of conflict, that it has a stake in the existence of men and institutions over which it has no power."[4] This is a point of fundamental importance. It is a messy point, to be sure. The judiciary can be corrupted by power. Universities, although they have often been havens of critical and independent thought, are also eager to serve power. But we do not live in a perfect world, nor will we. And the effort to invent and institutionalize truth-telling and independent judgment may be as good as we get.

To the judiciary and the academy, I would add "experts" generally and independent journalism specifically. A broad picture of how the party of factuality can be advanced is suggested in my concluding chapter concerning expert knowledge in a democracy, but the subtleties are worked out in the chapters on news. These chapters – all of them – suggest the dangers of simplification. Is news melodramatic? Sometimes it is. But is it normally melodramatic, as some critics say? Not at all, or so I argue in chapter 8, "The anarchy of events and the anxiety of story telling." Is news too focused on the immediate, the breaking story, the contingent? And does it offer too little analysis and interpretation? Perhaps. But contingencies – a massacre at My Lai in 1968, a break-in at the Watergate Democratic National Committee headquarters in 1972, a release of radiation at the Three Mile Island nuclear power plant in 1979, sadistic torture at Abu Ghraib prison in 2004 – may do more to alter thinking than even the best analysis and interpretation. Facts, events, contingencies humble our ideologies and theories and frameworks – at least they do if we have not blocked out the empirical world with dark glasses. (See chapter 5.)

Journalism is not a perfect vessel of truth. Its coverage of politics is based on unspoken, often unconscious, and sometimes unjustified assumptions (see chapter 6). Its narratives are based not only on a familiarity with the communities it covers but on an alienation from them (see chapters 3, 5, 6, and 7). Journalists are torn between understanding the world from the viewpoint of the sources they talk to – at the risk of being manipulated – and suspecting that their sources are lying or spinning – at the risk of cynicism. US journalism's obsession with facts and events often substitutes for a broader perspective and a historically or conceptually richer canvas. The distinctive strengths of American-style journalism (see chapter 3) are also weaknesses.

My late colleague, sociologist Bennett Berger, remarked to me years ago that the conclusion of most of my work is always the same: "Things are more complicated than you thought." I always wanted to prove Bennett wrong about this, but I have to acknowledge that he was onto something. This is not so terrible a confession; after all, about the only thing we can be sure of, regarding theories of the human condition, is that they are wrong. *All* of them are wrong, except those too empty or tautological to actually stand as theories at all. The good theories – those that actually provide some sort of non-tautological framework for seeing the world – are routinely upended by events (the special pleasure of journalism) or by variations across time (the revenge of historians) or across cultures (the revenge of anthropology) or by variations among individuals (the revenge of what statisticians call the "normal distribution").

Still, it is not enough to argue that journalism, public life, and public knowledge are complex. It is part of the scholar's job to blaze a useable trail through complexity. This requires having some idea about where you want the trail to take you. My goal is to understand journalism's special place in democracies, especially how to think through its mission once we stop equating democracy with maximum feasible participation or direct popular rule. Scholars, journalists, and citizens alike should learn to recognize the ways that institutions can help as well as hinder democratic government. We should learn to take seriously the benefits of representative democracy. We should learn that specialized knowledge (in experts) and concentrated power (in politicians or judges) are necessary ingredients in democracy and that the democratic task is to control the specialists rather than eliminate specialized knowledge. If we can learn all of this, we will be on a path to better understanding journalism's possibilities for democracy.

To affirm that there is something we can reliably refer to as a fact and to acknowledge that journalists are often the first to inform most of us about them is not to suppose that arriving at facts is easy. I hold only that seeking the truth is an inevitable choice for anyone dedicated to the values of a liberal society, that is, a society that refuses to rest complacently in a faith in anything except human fallibility. We are reminded of human fallibility over and over again since we can see in history scenes of the wreckage of lives destroyed by human folly and pride. In the face of this, no human institution seems worth our fidelity if it does not provide for its own monitoring, criticism, and revision. Institutions that do this seriously deserve our support; those who seek to weaken, marginalize, or destroy such institutions and who make decisions of fateful consequence on the basis of gut instinct and broad distrust of the accumulated knowledge of expert communities and popular judgment alike deserve our criticism – and should be voted out of power.

This is not to say experts are always right (even when they agree). It is certainly not to succumb to fantasies about how people are good at heart or about the wisdom of crowds or majorities – the Nuremberg rallies, the Roman coliseum, the popular lynchings in the American South? It is to say that people should approach the world as if leadership, thinking, deliberative effort, imagination, and recognition of facts can sometimes advance the cause of humanity.

In 1920 Walter Lippmann looked with distress upon the American journalism he was a part of. He believed journalism was incapable of reforming itself, that it did not have the intellectual resources to present an accurate picture of the world. If it succeeded – and he still hoped it might – it would be only because entities outside journalism – in government, in the universities, and in private organizations dedicated to investigation, analysis, and study, all of which he called "political observatories" – would come to provide predigested materials for reporters to relay to the public.[5] Lippmann did not believe the public would do very much with these materials – people could not absorb it all even if they wanted to, and for the most part people were just not sufficiently interested in the world beyond their doorstep to even bother. But, either from the political observatories directly or through reports of them in the news, government would come to operate with a more realistic vision of the world.

The problems of journalism today are of a different order. We see the deterioration of the economic structure that has sustained news gathering since the late nineteenth century. We see the erosion or demise of substantial local news organizations. The floundering of metropolitan daily newspapers is dire, but the picture is not all gloomy. First, the maturing of a more professional, detached, and analytical media since the 1960s has been impressive. Second, since the 1990s, there has been a vast, stunning multiplication on the Internet of the voices of civil society and exponents of media accountability. The rise of a global civil society, linked to the globalization of journalism itself, is powerful and transformative. There are many new journalistic voices (notably, bloggers) and new journalistic forms and forums (blogs, news aggregators, wikis, e-government sources). Meanwhile, conventional media that were once distributed locally have a new online presence that makes them nationally and globally available to hundreds of millions. In my judgment, historical studies of the press offer no grounds for nostalgia for the ghost of journalism past – nineteenth-century American newspapers were bitterly and wildly partisan in the cities, while the country papers were generally bland. Twentieth-century US journalism up to the late 1960s was less critical, less investigative, and more deferential to government office-holders than it is today, and significantly more narrow in its outlook (notably concerning women, minorities, gays and lesbians, and most topics a few steps away from government, politics, and the economy). The news was rarely enterprising in exploring topics not already on the agenda of leading law-makers.

No one can speak with much assurance about where journalism will move in the next quarter of a century or even the next ten years or the next five. Who, five years ago, would have predicted what a powerhouse Google has become? Who, five years ago, anticipated YouTube? Who imagined five years ago that bloggers would have gained such influence on the mainstream media? Or that Craigslist, that dates only to 1995 and was still just a blip on the national screen in 2001, would be the agent responsible for removing classified advertising as a mainstay of newspaper profitability? Or that Wikipedia would be so indispensable? Or that text in this visual and digital age, far from disappearing, would become a verb?

The chapters collected here take up diverse topics related to the news media and public life, but several themes stretch across them. Perhaps most important and most unusual in the literature about journalism is the theme that democracy in modern societies is representative democracy, and representative democracy has distinct virtues often obscured in a reflexive American populism. There is an old quip, "I would rather be governed by the first hundred people listed in the Boston phone book than by the Harvard faculty." Anyone who has sat through faculty meetings understands this sentiment, but neither alternative offered in the joke provides an adequate version of democracy. I do not want to be governed by the first 100 citizens of Boston or the first 100 faculty members at Harvard. I would rather be governed by the ten people selected in competitive elections by either the first 100 people in the Boston phone book or the first 100 members of the Harvard faculty. Representative democracy is not a "second best" solution we reluctantly resort to when the country's population grows too large. Representation creates a better system of governance – more honest, fair, and trustworthy – than direct democracy.

James Madison, father of the American Constitution, held this view. Like many of the Founders, Madison feared the direct influence of the people – that is, he feared the direct influence of property-owning white males who were not among the thoughtful, educated elite of their communities. His anxiety about popular democracy was not based on distrust of blacks, women, or the poor – these groups were simply not part of his calculations at all. But he believed the ordinary property-owning white male was provincial and ignorant, likely to be emotional and hot-headed, and unlikely to know what would suit the good of people from other communities and other walks of life.

In our own day, political theorist George Kateb has argued that representative democracy is superior in principle to direct or participatory democracy or, in Kateb's terms, Rousseauist government. In representative democracy, political authority is granted to those who wield it only temporarily (until the next election). Since it is granted temporarily, it becomes necessarily a chastened political authority. The public derives from this a sense of skepticism about authority and a sense of independence in relation to the powerful. In a Rousseauist world where decisions are made by the people at large, dissent (at least once a decision is made) becomes psychologically and socially difficult. In a representative democracy, compared to other political systems, dissent is relatively easy and, to a degree encouraged. Political authority is not only temporary but partial, because the representatives are leaders of a party in a system of two or more parties. This intensifies skepticism about power – "the very association of authority and partisanship promotes a sense of moral indeterminacy."[6] Kateb sums up his judgment as follows: "The main point here is that the existence of an electoral system . . . supplies a vivid, public, and continuous imparting of the moral lesson that the only tolerable authority is a deliberately chastened authority and that every effort must be made to have authority offend against moral equality as little as possible."[7]

Kateb makes a remarkable case. Of course, representative democracies do not in the short run avoid the temptations of unchastened power and it is entirely possible for elected governments to quash dissent, weaken the powers of opposition parties and intimidate putatively independent media, judges, universities, and experts. Still, over time, such efforts to consolidate rule in violation of democratic values typically come undone.

What would happen if journalists and journalism schools and journalistic self-understanding in general began to take representative democracy seriously and recognize in it the grounds for a revised model of journalism's place in democracy? The prevailing understanding of the function of the media in a democracy is that the people rule – more or less directly (and if they don't, they should) – and that they will rule more adequately if they are well informed by the press about public affairs. Journalism falls short of doing this job well because: (a) the government keeps information from the press or successfully manipulates the press into accepting its spin; (b) the corporate profit-oriented entities that gather most news are guided more by the economic advantages of sensation, sleaze, and the superficial than by efforts to inform the public; and (c) the professional journalists who work inside these corporate beasts and try to extract bits of truth from devious politicians are occupationally cautious, hobbled by in-group values of media elites, and motivated by professional advancement or driven by their own political views rather than by a passion to make democracy work.

This summarizes, I think, the lay understanding of how the press operates in the United States. Making some allowances for the greater role of public service broadcasting in much of western Europe, and for a stronger tradition of party-affiliated newspapers there, it is a rough approximation of European understandings, too. Although it is based on premises about democracy I do not accept, it may even have been a relatively adequate understanding of the news media half a century ago, but it seems a poor model now. This is so for several reasons. First, today there are many more organizations than just the conventional news media dedicated to informing citizens about public affairs in systematic and ongoing ways. Some of the most important of these new "news organizations" are bureaus and departments in the government itself. Second, new technologies have unleashed a plethora of new information-gathering and disseminating organizations – websites and other sources of authoritative information that have already had an impact, sometimes a shattering impact, on public affairs. Third, these same new technologies have helped to build an as-yet-unnamed quasi-public circulation of information that is altering the way people go about their lives. Think of the global impact of the digital photographs soldiers took of their own acts in abusing detainees at Abu Ghraib prison. In 2004, these photos came to light because of an inquiry initiated inside the US military, the technical ease of transmitting digital photography instantaneously across the globe, old-fashioned investigative reporting, competition among US media outlets to break the story and outrage in the Arab world and elsewhere that forced president George W. Bush to respond and thus validate the story as worthy of the front page.[8] In short, the whole "information ecology" of political and social life today is in the midst of profound change. The place of the press in this wider informational orbit must be re-described. These chapters can help toward that re-description, not by characterizing this new information ecology but by offering a view of democracy and a realistic portrait of news organizations that are necessary to making sense of it.

Democracy is not about maximizing popular involvement in decision-making. It is about assuring a role for popular participation and for popular

review of governmental performance within a system of competitive elections, due process, the protection of individual rights, the protection of
freedoms of speech, press, petition, and association, and the preservation
of a pluralistic culture. In this context, the press should be understood as
multiform and multipurpose, a mixed-bag of an institution. There is nothing
pure or refined about it. It is the same organization that sells consumers
investigative reporting, the weather, recipes, and crossword puzzles in a
single daily bundle. It is the same organization that may take great pains
in one section to be even-handed and detached, say, in covering candidates
for political office, and in another section cover the local sports team with
partisan fervor and, when the team is winning, evident glee. And I am still
talking about a single news product, not the differences among different
news organizations that may conceive their tasks in quite different ways
from one another.

Different features of news serve different democratic functions. The
blogger does not usually gather news but criticizes those who do. The
front-line reporter and the blogger can both be useful. The blogger obviously feeds on the reporter but we now have more than a few cases where
mainstream news reports feed off of tips, ideas, and insights initiated in
the blogosphere. The investigative reporter is the star of a watchdog press,
but that does not mean that the obituary writer at the same organization is
not also serving democracy, telling us something about what life and death
mean in our day. The obituaries honor and validate a community, a village,
or a nation. They celebrate achievement and they may remind us that even
the high and mighty have been lonely or sick or sad. The investigative
reporter, the White House correspondent, the business reporter, the theater
critic, the obit writer are all offering news that serves vital social – and
democratic – functions.

Given this complexity – there is that word again – a lot of familiar talk
of what the media are and how they operate, and how they serve or fail to
serve democracy, is tendentious, simple-minded, or just mistaken. From
journalists, too often talk about the media is self-congratulatory or defen-
sive; from external critics, too often the talk is innocent of realities in the
daily practices of journalism and too likely to pick and choose the examples that illustrate a pre-conceived thesis. It is a big world out there in our
garrulous news media and there is scarcely any thesis without a set of
examples to illustrate it! The task I have set myself is to try to know the
world of journalism not as journalists know it, but with what journalists
know about it in mind and how journalists experience their work and their
world in view. I try to picture how a question looks from the perspective
of the reporter in the field or the editor in the newsroom. I have never been
either – but I have talked to both, I have occasionally observed both at

work, and I have often heard them discuss the work they do at conferences or in print.

My outlook offers a kind of humility on behalf of, but also in contention with, academic inquiry. We learn from our own inadequacies at comprehensive analysis not to accept any position that tells us the game is over, that the world can't get better, because, say, the corporations have the politicians in their pockets, or because the corporations run the media, or because technologies dictate certain outcomes, or because capitalism is an unstoppable and dangerous dynamo, or because ethnic and racial hatred runs deeper even than capitalism. Of course, one would have to be crazy not to acknowledge the power of technology and money and hate. But if that's all there is, we would not have witnessed since the 1950s a civil rights revolution, a transformative women's movement, and the fall of communism. As human beings, we have the capacity to exceed ourselves and to violate our own best predictions.

I am generally an optimist, but some of these chapters have a slightly elegiac tone, particularly chapter 4. This chapter began as part of a lecture series at the San Diego Museum of Art, built around a major exhibit of the art of Norman Rockwell. It focuses on the newspaper – not news more broadly, but the newspaper form itself. The tone of loss and remembrance is hard to escape when that form is perhaps today in its twilight, or at the least is a long way from the dominating behemoth of public culture that it was a century ago. The newspaper and the wire services remain the original sources of the lion's share of public affairs news today (television, radio, and online news sources remain parasitic on the original reporting that newspaper organizations still undertake). At the same time, newspapers share the field of public information with more other entities than ever – Walter Lippmann's "political observatories" now play vital roles. These are polling organizations, non-partisan advocacy organizations, and organizations that gather facts in pursuit of partisan objectives through research or through lawsuits. Sometimes they are employees of the government itself – for instance, the inspectors-general in many US federal departments and agencies whose statutory task includes investigating and auditing the agencies in which they are located and reporting their findings to the Congress and the president. Their work frequently uncovers waste, mismanagement, fraud, and sometimes illegal activities that provide the grounds for lawsuits, legislation, or simply the public embarrassment of scandal and subsequent Congressional inquiry. Democracies need not only an unlovable press but a self-divided government, one that has managed to find ways – inadequate and incomplete like all human institutions, but invaluable nonetheless – to direct attention to disagreeable facts.

Despite the significant growth of these alternative information sources, they are still translated into public currency through the work of the press. Should newspapers pass from the scene (rather than passing from ink on paper to pixels on screens), democracy would be in grave danger. Democracies still need the press and particularly require an unlovable press. They need journalists who get in the face of power – and are enabled to do so because both their doggedness and their irreverence is protected by law, by a conducive political culture, and by a historical record of having served self-government well when they hunt down elusive or hidden facts. Democracy works better if we can guarantee journalists what Arendt called "the standpoint outside the political realm – outside the community to which we belong and the company of our peers." This standpoint, she wrote, is "one of the various modes of being alone," and she listed among outstanding "modes of truthtelling" the following: "the solitude of the philosopher, the isolation of the scientist and the artist, the impartiality of the historian and the judge, and the independence of the fact-finder, the witness, and the reporter."[9]

Isn't it interesting that she should put "the reporter" in a place of honor, bringing up the rear in that sentence? Often the first to bring us news and to arrest into memorable language or image some disturbing nugget of factuality, the reporter holds a special place among those who commit themselves to seeking the truths that self-governing people depend on.

2

Six or seven things news can do for democracy

Democracy and journalism are not the same thing. Most of the key philosophical works that lay out a case for democracy or a theory of democracy make no reference to journalism. This is not, of course, surprising – there was no journalism in ancient Greece. Even when the thinkers around the American and French revolutions were making their arguments for republican government in pamphlets and in the pages of weekly newspapers, the press played little role in their calculations.

Later, and with growing assurance through the years, journalists themselves have insisted that their work is essential to the public good. Their self-promotion, along with what came to be the self-evident importance of freedom of expression in any society claiming to be a liberal democracy, made journalism's role in democracy seem obvious. One prominent American scholar of journalism, James Carey, concluded that journalism and democracy are one and the same, that "journalism as a practice is unthinkable except in the context of democracy; in fact, journalism is usefully understood as another name for democracy."[1]

This takes the plea for journalism's democratic virtue a step too far. That journalism is crucial to modern democracy seems clear; that it is not by any means sufficient to democracy seems equally clear; that journalism does not by itself produce or provide democracy seems likewise apparent. Professor Carey offers a normative – one could even say, a romantic – notion of journalism, defined as a pursuit so intrinsically democratic at heart that it does not exist if democracy does not exist. Reality is more complicated and less happy. If we accept common understandings of journalism as the practice of periodically producing and publicly disseminating information and commentary about contemporary affairs of general public interest and importance, then journalism existed in Chile in the 1980s when democracy did not, and it existed in Franco's Spain without democracy, and it exists in China today, sometimes even daring to criticize the government – but without bringing China appreciably closer to democratic political institutions. Journalism exists and has long existed outside democracy.

Democracy does not necessarily produce journalism nor does journalism necessarily produce democracy. British journalism arose in a monarchy. American journalism, a journalism of colonial territories under a monarchical, colonial power, preceded American democracy. Where there *is* democracy, however, or where there are forces prepared to bring it about, journalism can provide a number of different services to help establish or sustain representative government. The relative importance of these different services changes over time and varies across democracies. With the digital age upon us and changes taking place in journalism everywhere, the democratic functions which journalism serves or the ways it serves them will change again.

But what are these functions? There is little clarity about this, despite all the talk of journalism's great gifts to democratic society. Taking inventory of what journalism offers to democracy, or what, in different times and places, it has provided, is a task long overdue. I see six primary functions that news has served or can serve in a democracy – and a seventh, generally ignored, that news could and should serve. (I will get to that later.) The six functions journalism has frequently assumed in democratic societies, in different combinations and with different emphases, are:

I   information: the news media can provide fair and full information so citizens can make sound political choices;

II   investigation: the news media can investigate concentrated sources of power, particularly governmental power;

III analysis: the news media can provide coherent frameworks of interpretation to help citizens comprehend a complex world;

IV   social empathy: journalism can tell people about others in their society and their world so that they can come to appreciate the viewpoints and lives of other people, especially those less advantaged than themselves;

V   public forum: journalism can provide a forum for dialogue among citizens and serve as a common carrier of the perspectives of varied groups in society;

VI   mobilization: the news media can serve as advocates for particular political programs and perspectives and mobilize people to act in support of these programs.

These different functions are sometimes at cross purposes. In particular, the mobilization or advocacy function may undermine the reliability of the informational and investigative functions. Still, it is not unusual for a single news organ, particularly a newspaper, to serve democracy in all these ways at once.

I Informing the public

The most familiar claim about journalism in a democracy is that it informs the citizens. Here journalism's function is educational, informing the public – the ultimate democratic authority – of what its political representatives are doing, what dangers and opportunities for society loom on the horizon, and what fellow citizens are up to, for better and for worse. The educational function of journalism puts the public in the front seat and enables the citizenry to participate in self-government.

Much of the power of the media comes from the simple fact that news tells us things we would not otherwise know. Obvious as this may be, it has not always been taken for granted. Democracy probably has done more to make information a part of journalism than journalism has done to make information a part of democracy. In the eighteenth century, even representative legislatures and assemblies operated largely in secret from the people who elected them. Reporters in the middle of the eighteenth century in Britain might talk to MPs as they left the House of Commons, but they could not themselves observe the MPs debate. In Samuel Johnson's parliamentary reporting, for instance, most of the speakers sounded in style very much the same and discoursed at length on Johnson's own favorite topics. In a word, he invented – he had no other choice – the news.[2] The United States Senate met entirely in secret for its first few years, as did the US Constitutional Convention before it. Freedom of the press at that time meant – and this was not a small thing – freedom for a writer to speak his opinion as he wished, even in criticism of the government. But it did not mean a freedom to report. It did not guarantee access to government offices or government officials. As late as 1842, John Quincy Adams, former president, wrote in his diary with disgust that President Tyler's sons "divulged all his cabinet secrets to . . . hired reporters for Bennett's HERALD newspaper in New York."[3] The need for the adjective "hired" to modify "reporters" suggests how novel and disreputable the occupation of reporting was at that time.

Even several generations later, when reporting had become established, some of the tools of the journalistic trade elicited disapproval. The most notable of these was interviewing, a practice that became widely accepted in the United States by the 1880s, but that was judged unseemly in much of Europe until after World War I. A French observer in the 1880s criticized "the spirit of inquiry and espionage" of the American reporters. He attacked "the mania for interviewing" and predicted that the British, much more sensible than the Americans or the French, would never accept it. A more admiring Danish journalist at the same time noted of the American press, "The reporter and the interview are the focus of these papers . . . this is ideal journalism. These papers are produced by journalists, not aesthetes and politicians, and they are written for the lower class to help them, inform them and fight corruption for them." This overestimates the power and purpose of the interview; the interview became, after all, a tool of politicians and celebrities – and journalists – for self-advancement, more than a point of entry into political life for the masses. Still, interviewing, like reporting in general, seemed a practice fit for a democratic society. The informational function of journalism is consonant with democratic social and cultural style. American journalists of the late nineteenth century were simply more brash and more raw in their manners than Europeans. They were not part of a literary circle. They presented themselves as men of the street and the city, not as men of the salon.

II   Investigation

In the second function of journalism in a democracy, the governors on stage and not the governed in the auditorium are the focus and journalism is watching them. News becomes a theater in which conflicts inside government are played out – regardless of whether the public audience is large or small. Journalism performs its institutional role as a watchdog even if nobody in the provinces is following the news. All that matters is that people in government believe that some people somewhere are following the news. All that is necessary to inspire this belief is that an inner circle of attentive citizens is watchful. This is sufficient to produce in the leaders a fear of public embarrassment or public discrediting, public controversy, legal prosecution, or fear of losing an election. The job of the media, in this respect, is to make powerful people tremble.

There are two different versions of this dynamic. One emphasizes that news inspires fear of publicity among powerful leaders and the other focuses on how news inspires thinking, reflection, debate, and engagement among highly attentive elites. In the latter sense, this may be the democratic function that most nearly approaches the Habermasian ideal of a "public sphere." Victor Navasky, long-time publisher of the liberal weekly *The Nation*, notes that Frank Walsh, a US senator in the 1920s, wrote articles about the railroads for the Hearst newspaper chain, reaching some 10 million people – but the articles evoked no public response. Walsh published the same material in *The Nation*, circulation 27,000, and reported: "The day *The Nation* went on the Washington newsstands my telephone started ringing. I heard from editors, broadcasters and Congressmen."[4] How many readers may not matter as much as which readers they are and, as Navasky suggests, how intensely and instrumentally they read.

The watchdog function of the press is negative: it is designed to foil tyranny rather than to forward new movement or new policy; it prevents bad things from happening or continuing rather than advancing the cause of the good. Here nothing about journalism matters more than its obligation to hold government officials to the legal and moral standards of public service. Public officials should try to do what they say they will try to do. They should refrain from using office for private gain. They should live up to their oaths of office. They should make good on their campaign promises. And if democracy is to work, the public should be well informed of just what these people do while in office and how well they live up to their legal obligations, campaign promises, and public avowals. The media therefore should investigate.

Investigating to keep government officials honest is not inconsistent with informing to keep the general public knowledgeable, but it is not the same thing. The ideal of informing the public objectively and with fairness seems to presume that the world is relatively simple and open and displays itself to the journalist whose job is to describe that visible world without fear or favor. The ideal of protecting democracy through investigation is different. It assumes that the world is relatively complex and veiled, and that some of the information that is most important to citizens is embedded in opaque structures and systems and may in fact be deliberately hidden from view. The world is not an open book. It is a text of many texts, written for many purposes, and some of the texts are intentionally written over other texts to obscure them. The journalists therefore have an obligation to affirmatively seek the text behind the text, the story behind the story. Journalists should be judged not only by fairness in reporting but by energy in detection. In this model of journalism, the world is not so much a complicated place that needs fair-minded description and analysis as a misleading and deceptive wall of pretense that must be breached by a professional truth-teller. If the virtues of the informative journalist are observation and judgment, the virtues of the investigative journalist are persistence and suspicion.

Suspicion would seem an easy virtue to cultivate. It is not. If it had been left to the top reporters at the *Washington Post* to pursue the Watergate story, it would have been dropped. The star reporters all believed that

Richard Nixon and his chief aides were too smart to get caught up in dirty tricks and burglaries. All of them were wrong. It is not so easy to maintain one's suspicion. It is also not easy to turn suspicion on one's friends. The 2006 Pulitzer Prize for national reporting went to the *San Diego Union-Tribune*, among the more conservative newspapers in the country. The *Union-Tribune* routinely endorsed (if without notable enthusiasm) Republican Congressman Randy "Duke" Cunningham from his first campaign on through each re-election bid. But it was this newspaper that followed up Cunningham's suspicious sale of his home to a defense contractor who then mysteriously sold it for a $700,000 loss.

The reporters wanted to know why. What they unearthed was the worst bribery scandal in the history of the United States Congress. Mr. Cunningham is now serving an eight-year term in prison, and the ardently conservative *Union-Tribune* took pride in sending a stalwart conservative to prison.[5]

III   Analysis

Journalists aid democracy when they explain a complicated event or process in a comprehensible narrative. Today this is sometimes called "explanatory journalism," and explanatory journalism has its own Pulitzer Prize category. The virtue required for analytic journalism is intelligence and a kind of pedagogical flair, linking the capacity to understand a complex situation with a knack for transmitting that understanding to a broad public. Explanatory journalism might try to illustrate a complicated social phenomenon through the life of a single individual. A lead story in the *New York Times* (March 26, 2007) came from Conrad, Montana, and described Mary Rose Derks, an 81-year-old widow with a long-term-care health insurance policy that denied her coverage, despite her dementia. Not until the sixth paragraph does it become clear that the story is not about Mary Derks but about the scandalous long-term-care insurance industry. To produce this one story, the *Times* reviewed 400 cases of elderly policyholders who "confront unnecessary delays and overwhelming bureaucracies."[6] Strong analysis, like sound investigation, requires something that simply providing information does not require so fully: money. It takes a great deal of time and effort to do serious analysis.

Consider one *New York Times* report on the consequences for personal security in Baghdad of the "surge" in US troops in Iraq in 2007. Two days before General David Petraeus, commander of the US forces in Iraq, testified to the US Congress about the effects of the surge, the *Times* published a detailed report on how it had affected three demographically disparate neighborhoods of Baghdad. For two months, reporters spent over half of their working days on this story, and they were backed up with the efforts of 29 other reporters, photographers, and editors. Their editor spent two weeks of her time working on the story: "Just to maintain a bureau in Iraq these days, between life insurance and blast walls, guards and transportation, guns and generators, takes more than $3 million annually at the *Times* – plus staff salaries."[7]

Few news organizations are willing to invest so much in journalism, and as newspapers' economic prospects worsen under the impact of alternative entertainment, news, and advertising sources, this poses a serious threat to public investigation and analysis. Online journalism, particularly online journalism that is not sponsored by major print and television media, has so far shown little capacity for, or interest in, making the kind of large investments in investigation and analysis that make conventional media, especially newspapers, invaluable for democracy.

Who is addressed in explanatory journalism? Both the attentive public and a potential attentive public. What may not be obvious is how valuable this journalism is to the attentive public, those who are already well informed. An individual well informed about foreign policy may nonetheless be naïve about domestic policy; someone familiar with problems in social service delivery for children may know little or nothing about social services for the elderly. Explanatory journalism articulates a silence or foregrounds what was background, making it thereby available for conversation and collective notice.

IV   Social empathy

What I am calling "social empathy" has little place in the familiar rhetoric about journalism. It deserves more attention. My own thinking about this goes back to a conference I attended in 1980 where Roger Wilkins, a distinguished journalist, then an editor at the *Washington Star*, told a story about sitting down at a lunch counter next to an elderly black woman in Washington and striking up a conversation with her. I do not remember the story precisely but it was something like this. Wilkins, himself African-American, asked the woman which candidate she favored in the upcoming presidential election: "President Carter, he's a good man. I don't know about this Ronald Reagan." So, are you going to vote? "Oh, no, I don't vote." Why is that? "Too busy and too tired, it's too much trouble."

Why did Wilkins bring that story to this conference of academics and journalists discussing the role of the press in democracy? Because, he said, he did not think journalism could do anything to change the views or actions of the woman at the lunch counter. But he did think journalism could tell her story. Journalism could inform those of us who do vote, and those of us who have the power to make decisions and the leverage to turn society in one direction or another, about that woman and others like her so that we could see her and understand her with compassion.[8]

I think journalism does more of this and does it better than it ever has. Coverage of Hurricane Katrina was rich, passionate, and compassionate in many news outlets. With the *New York Times*, it was also persistent. The *Times* assigned a "Katrina editor" and followed up the disaster with story after story, nearly every week, for the next year, with continuing coverage long after that, following the story not only in New Orleans and along the Gulf Coast but in Houston and Atlanta and other communities where hurricane victims relocated. Human interest stories have been a part of journalism for a long time but they are used more and more instrumentally these days, to draw readers or viewers into a larger tale, one that tells us not just about an interesting or unusual individual but shows us how that person's experience links up with larger issues. The sociologist C. Wright Mills defined what he called "the sociological imagination" as the leap of mind that shows the connection between a person's "private troubles" and the "public issues" that gave rise to them.[9] The journalistic imagination is similar. The better news organizations of our day make a great effort to demonstrate the link between private troubles and public issues.

Social empathy is a surprisingly recent development in journalism. In the United States, exposés of "how the other half lives" go back at least to the work of Jacob Riis (who gave us the phrase) and Nellie Bly in the late nineteenth century. Their work drew attention to categories of people (the poor or the insane) while today's journalistic empathy goes out not just to large, publicly relevant, demographically defined or bureaucratically demarcated groups, but to individuals and groups and slivers of groups who may have no public face or public identity. At some point in the 1970s or a bit later, "the personal is political," a slogan of the women's movement, became a journalistic cliché. Personal trouble as entrée to a public issue seemed almost inescapable by the 1980s. Using human interest to open up larger public issues would seem to be a literary device as old as the hills, but, in the American media at least, it is not. Introducing the general significance of a particular public issue by examining an individual case, a person whose troubles are related to or are an instance of a public problem, became a familiar part of the journalistic idiom in the 1970s and 1980s.[10] In the *New York Times'* coverage of the long aftermath of Hurricane Katrina, a series of follow-up stories over the ensuing year focused on a single block of the very poor, largely African-American neighborhood, the Lower 9th Ward.

The practice of linking individual vignettes to large public policy issues became a matter of public controversy in the early Reagan years. In 1982, CBS television presented a Bill Moyers-narrated documentary that tried to examine the impact of Reagan's budget reductions on the lives of everyday citizens. The program focused on four individuals adversely affected by Reagan's cuts in government spending. David Gergen, then Reagan's communications director, attacked the documentary for blaming poverty on the president.

But the president, himself widely noted for using anecdotes – sometimes fabricated – to make a point, was already exercised about this kind of journalism-by-anecdote. He said, "You can't turn on the evening news without seeing that they're going to interview someone else who has lost his job. Is it news that some fellow out in South Succotash someplace has just been laid off and that he should be interviewed nationwide?" All of this resides in the collective memory of social science because Shanto Iyengar and Donald Kinder tested the so-called "vividness hypothesis" in the laboratory. This hypothesis is simply that the more vivid, dramatic, or emotionally compelling the text or image people are exposed to, the more it will influence them, affecting their opinions or enduring in their memories. But, surprisingly, Iyengar and Kinder found that "news stories that direct viewers' attention to the flesh and blood victims of national problems prove no more persuasive than news stories that cover national problems impersonally – indeed, they tend to be less persuasive."

Iyengar and Kinder find their results mysterious. They speculate: perhaps viewers blame the victims and see them as causes of their own misfortune; perhaps viewers get so caught up in the melodrama of the specific instance that they fail to make the sociological leap that, for more sophisticated viewers, is so obviously what the journalists are up to; or perhaps the journalist's implicit or explicit subordinate thesis – these people are just like you or, more spiritually, there but for the grace of God are you – is something viewers simply do not accept: "I am not black. I am not old. My family has not abandoned me. I have never relied on government assistance. I do not live in New Jersey. So what you are showing me does not translate into my own everyday life."[11]

Social empathy stories, then, do not always prompt the imaginative leap in readers and viewers that journalists intend. Still, it seems one of the great achievements of the leading contemporary press and one that is linked closely to democratic values. It expresses the virtues of curiosity and empathy in the journalist and it encourages empathy and understanding in the audience. Joseph Raz, a political philosopher, writes that it is important in a democracy, and particularly a pluralistic democratic society, for the media to portray and thereby legitimate various styles of life in society, giving them "the stamp of public acceptability."[12] Learning about our neighbors through the mass media, both news and entertainment, Raz briefly but elegantly suggests, serves a vital democratic function. Reporters who do this work surely recognize that they are serving democracy, but journalists as well as media critics who urge news to serve democracy better rarely call attention to this sort of journalism, often not at all directly political.

True, covering medicine and education and religion – topics through which we may learn about and acquire empathy for people different from ourselves – blurs into coverage of dieting, restaurants, cars, celebrities, and other fluffy topics of a self-absorbed society and can be a distraction from public life rather than an expansion of it. Still, all of these topics are potentially doors into public life. (Physician Barron Lerner's instructive study of media presentations of famous people with serious illnesses offers good examples of how the public's frequently disparaged fascination with celebrities becomes an avenue to useful public education.)[13]

V Public forum

From the early days of journalism to the present, newspapers have made space for letters to the editor. In the United States since the 1970s, leading newspapers also have provided an "op-ed" page – so named because it is the page opposite the editorial page – in which staff writers, syndicated columnists, and guest columnists, experts as well as ordinary citizens, provide a variety of views on current issues. More US newspapers feel a responsibility to provide a range of views in their pages because few major cities these days have more than one daily newspaper.

Television provides little help in extending the public forum function of news. Television news still tends to convey a naïve impression that there is only one way to see the world – Walter Cronkite used to close his CBS News broadcasts, "And that's the way it is." That is still largely the way it is in television news, although there is more room than there used to be for a degree of spontaneity and subjectivity in the live reports from journalists in the field.[14] If one looks more broadly at cable television, various opinion shows have advanced this "public forum" function of journalism. Opinion, perspective, passion, and anger, even if it is often more theatrical than sincere, have enlivened the TV screen. The most popular and pervasive of the voices, however, are politically conservative – the public forum on cable television and on talk radio is more lively than it used to be, but it is also skewed sharply to the right.

The public forum function of journalism has cracked wide open with the creation of the World Wide Web; the Internet opens up this journalistic function in the most wide-ranging and profound way. Its virtue is not individual but social, the virtue of interaction, of conversation, of an easy and agreeable democratic sociability.

VI Mobilization

Historically, no form of journalism has been more important than partisan journalism. Even in US journalism, widely recognized for its powerful commitment to notions of non-partisanship and objectivity, party-based journalism dominated the past. Partisan journalism seeks to rally only those who share the journalist's political or ideological position. This was the dominant concept of journalism in the United States throughout the nineteenth century.

Why was the partisan press so pervasive? Not because the press failed in an effort to be fair and balanced; the nineteenth-century press rarely tried to be fair or balanced. Newspapers were subsidized by political parties directly and indirectly. The publishers, editors, and reporters understood their job to be political cheerleading and mobilizing, not political reporting. As one historian puts it, nineteenth-century newspapers were much more interested in reaching citizens' feet than in influencing their minds, eager to get them into the streets marching, parading, and going to vote rather than to persuade them by argument or facts or reasoning to share an opinion, let alone to think for themselves.[15] Top editors looked forward to political appointments if their party captured the White House.

Was there information in nineteenth-century newspapers? Yes, there was, but it was doggedly partisan. The press did not at that time endorse either of the first two democratic functions of journalism I have discussed in a way familiar to Americans today. The intent of the newspapers was not to create an informed citizen but a party-loyal citizen. The intent was not to reveal government scandal but to reveal government scandal if and only if the opposition party controlled the government.

There is much to be said for this model of journalism as partisan cheerleader and propagandist, dedicated to exhortation and incitement to participate. If different partisan viewpoints are well represented among news institutions, then a journalist-as-advocate model may serve the public interest well. Partisan journalism enlists the heart as well as the mind of the audience. It gives readers and viewers not only information but a cause. In contrast, the objective, information-providing and non-partisan investigative functions of today's leading news organizations may have de-mobilizing effects. They provide people with information but they do not advise people what to do with it. If anything, they seem to imply that nothing can be done, that politicians are only interested in their own political careers. The undertone of cynicism in news reports may be a factor in encouraging an undertone of cynicism in the general public.[16]

If the partisan press was so pervasive in the nineteenth-century United States, where did the modern American idea of news as a professional, balanced resource for an informed citizenry come from? This is a long story.[17] But, in short, it begins with reformers at the end of the nineteenth century who attacked party politics. These reformers sought to make elections "educational." They sponsored civil service reform rather than filling government jobs with loyal party workers. In a variety of ways, they tried to insulate the independent, rational citizen from the distorting enthusiasms of party. In the 1880s, political campaigns began to shift from parades to pamphlets, and so put a premium on literacy. Newspapers broke free. The attractions of the marketplace captured more and more newspapers – a danger, to be sure, but a danger that freed the press from subservience to the parties. In the 1890s, the Australian ballot system swept the nation and so for the first time in American history literacy was required to cast a ballot. The novelty of the Australian ballot was that the state took responsibility for printing ballots that listed the candidates from all parties that qualified for the election. This meant that voters received their ballots from state election officials at the polling place, not from party workers en route to the polling place; it meant that the voter had to make a choice of candidates by marking the ballot; and it normally meant that provision was made for the voter to mark the ballot in secret. With this innovation, voting changed from a social and public duty to a private right, from a social obligation to party enforceable by social pressure to a civic obligation or abstract loyalty, enforceable only by private conscience. In the early 1900s, a variety of reforms from non-partisan municipal elections to the initiative and referendum, in which citizens voted for or against the enactment of specific laws, imposed more challenging cognitive tasks on prospective voters than ever before. These changes enshrined "the informed citizenry" in the US political imagination.[18]

Between 1880 and 1910, the most basic understandings of American politics were challenged. Reformers invented the language by which Americans still judge politics. It stresses being informed while it dismisses or demeans parties and partisanship. To put this more pointedly, the political party, the single most important agency ever invented for mass political participation, is the institution that current civic talk and current civic education regularly abhor and that is rendered almost invisible in the way Americans conduct the actual process of voting. Insofar as the way people *do* vote follows a set of enduring instructions to them about the way they *should* vote and the way they should think about voting, the civic lesson of election day as the United States has organized it for the past century recommends contempt for parties and partisanship.

Most nineteenth-century electoral rhetoric was not about informed choice but about loyalty and fraternity. In contrast, US electoral rhetoric in the twentieth century, and since, insists that people make their choices among candidates, parties, and issues. Independent, reasoned choice is the ideal. Non-partisan groups like the League of Women Voters encourage everyone to vote. Non-partisan groups also try to elevate the moral quality of politics by placing emphasis on analysis of the issues. In California, the state provides every registered voter with an extensive printed information guide, routinely over 100 pages of dense print. In Oregon in 2000, the voter information guide was so long it had to be printed in two volumes.

This does not mean people are in fact well informed. But it does mean that the collective ritual of getting the news in the press and obtaining information from other sources over the past century has been very different from what it was in the century before.

VII   Publicizing representative democracy

There is – at least, there should be – a seventh function for the news media in a democracy. I did not see this until reading a thoughtful essay by Kent Asp, "Fairness, Informativeness and Scrutiny: The Role of News Media in Democracy," a set of reflections based on studies of the Swedish media. Although there is much in this essay that I found instructive, I found myself in sharp disagreement when Asp offered his most general formulation of the function of news in a democracy: "In a democracy media should work for the realization of the will of the people by facilitating the free exchange of ideas."[19] Instantly I wanted to add, "within a system of free and fair elections and with protection of civil liberties and human rights." I wanted, in other words, a role for journalism that was democratic but not populist, that regarded and respected constitutionalism and championed a strong role in representative democracies for the protection of minority rights. I wanted Asp to be skeptical about the notion "the will of the people." "Realization of the will of the people" does not provide the best government, even assuming one had some reliable means (which we do not) of determining what that will is. No means that I can imagine for ascertaining and then realizing the people's will can provide as fair and just a system as a mixed mode of government with constitutional protections in place. Even this messy arrangement I am advocating can and does misfire. No system is immune to damage from deceit, avarice, or even so moderate a sin as chumminess.

But what role can journalism play in advancing some version of liberal democracy, as I would wish, rather than a majoritarian democracy as such? Journalists have not articulated a broad normative function for their craft in these terms. Perhaps the task of living up to the first six functions of news in a democracy is more than enough without journalists dedicating themselves to teaching political philosophy and encouraging a fuller, richer vision of liberal democracy than one normally finds in public life when politicians pander to populist sentiments. Still, to the extent that journalists or scholars who study journalism articulate democratic virtues while ignoring or subordinating liberal and constitutional virtues, journalism's role in democracy is left unmoored.

I do not suggest that journalists become evangelists for a more sophisticated understanding of representative democracy – except, perhaps, on the editorial page. What I propose is that greater sophistication about representative democracy should lead journalists to cover more carefully some institutions and relationships that today they take for granted or ignore. In the United States, the past 40 years have seen significant growth in institutions of government transparency – open records laws at state and local levels, for instance, and the Freedom of Information Act nationally. There has also been growth in a variety of systems of accountability in government and in politics, including the Federal Elections Commission that requires candidates for national office to disclose the amount and source of campaign contributions; the Government Accountability Office that takes responsibility for the fiscal accountability of federal agencies; the inspectors-general assigned to many federal agencies and responsible for reporting to the president and the Congress on investigations of the propriety and lawfulness of a wide variety of agency actions. For instance, the inspector-general of the Department of Justice produced a report critical of the FBI's failures in tracking the men who, on September 11, 2001, committed the bloody acts of terrorism in New York and Washington.

All of these government officials help provide a set of informational checks and balances within the government, but none of them are widely known to the general public or mentioned in our schools or highlighted in the media. Yet the ways in which democratic government is held accountable operate not only through "vertical accountability" – a direct accounting to the public through elections – but through "horizontal accountability" in which one branch of government holds another branch accountable.[20]

These are not just details. They are the ways democracy works – or fails to work. Voter turnout is a matter of great interest to US journalists and a matter of great concern to all who worry over the health of US democracy, but the vigor of horizontal accountability should be of interest once one recognizes that liberal democracy is not plebiscitarian and that representative government today operates through a large executive branch that the press by itself is in no position to monitor closely.

Conclusion

Where will journalism be in 10 or 20 or 50 years? No one knows. We do know that it will be more online than it is today. It will be more online next week! I think we can be confident that some varieties of television news will continue, and radio news will continue. There are more concerns about newspapers, it is fair to say, but at this point there is no online news gathering organization of any scope and substance that is not a part of a print-based (*New York Times*, *Washington Post*, or others) or TV-based (CNN or BBC or others) media organization. There are all sorts of bloggers, all sorts of aggregators, all sorts of opinion columnists whose presence exists only online, and many of them are making impressive contributions to public discourse and to several of the democratic functions discussed in this chapter. But none of them has invested in news gathering in the way that hundreds of newspaper publishers have done. The efforts of these newspapers cannot be dispensed with, even though the economic model that sustains them has to be redesigned.

With the arrival of the Web and the growth of the blogosphere, the public forum and mobilizing functions of journalism have grown relative to the informing and investigative and social empathy functions. The Web also helps create an incipient new function of journalism for democracy, one in which the divide between the journalist and the audience for journalism disappears. Some people talk about this as "citizen journalism." It has always existed to a degree. Every time a citizen calls up a news organization and says "I have a hot tip for you," this is citizen journalism. Every letter to the editor is citizen journalism. But now citizens can simply go online and publish the tip or the letter on their own.[21] This is a new self-organizing journalism, already making waves, already enacting something new and exciting.

The present sea-change in the mass media does not herald the end of journalism, but newspapers are in for a very rough ride and some of them, even some very distinguished ones, will not survive. The informative, investigative, and social empathy functions that journalism has sometimes offered democracy may get redistributed across different journalistic and non-journalistic organizations. They may not be as centrally concentrated in newspapers and television networks as they once were. In the long run, this is not something to fear. It is something to work with and it should immeasurably advance the information resources of citizens, professional journalists, political activists, and others (including, of course, enemies as well as friends of democratic government). We should be open to its possibilities and recognize that the unruliness of a decentralized and multi-voiced informational system may be among democracy's greatest assets.

Journalism does not produce democracy where democracy does not exist, but it can do more to help democracies thrive if it recognizes the multiple services it affords self-government, encourages the virtues that underwrite those services, and clarifies for journalists and the public the many gifts news contributes to democratic aspirations.

3

The US model of journalism: exception or exemplar?

American journalism began, like American politics, as a version of British institutions. American printers in the eighteenth century imported their presses, type, and ink from Britain, and borrowed most of their news directly from London papers. For the first half-century of American newspapers, readers could find little local news; the American colonies were an outpost of a British world, and the papers demonstrated closer connections to London than to neighboring colonies or even to their own sites of publication.

There is still much that links the British and American models of the press, but there is also much that separates them: the relative importance of news in the capital and in provincial regions, the degree of connection between press and party, a more clearly bifurcated "quality press" and "popular press" distinction in Britain than in the United States, the presence (in Britain) and absence (in America) of a strong tradition of public service broadcasting, and the greater legal protection for American journalism than for British journalism, thanks to jealously guarded First Amendment privileges.

What follows is an account of how distinctive features of American journalism emerged, particularly "boosterism," the inclination of news organizations as business establishments to sing the praises, overlook the faults, and promote the economic growth of their home towns; professionalization under the banner of objectivity; and staunch adherence to the freedoms provided by the First Amendment. I will reflect on some of the positive and negative consequences of these features for sustaining democratic society, and will consider whether the unique features of the American system of news make it useful or ill suited as a model for journalism elsewhere around the globe.

Boosterism and the American press

Journalism is not one of the venerable professions. Certainly it was not well established when Benjamin Franklin's older brother James began printing the second newspaper in Britain's American colonies in 1720. James Franklin's friends tried to dissuade him, saying they thought the paper not likely to succeed, "one newspaper being in their judgment enough for America."[1] But James, like so many American entrepreneurs who followed him, plunged ahead nonetheless, driven not by shrewd calculation of "what America needs" but by what personal ambition and ego recommended and which local opportunities seemed to beckon.

Commercial motives propelled American journalism from its beginnings. Still, in the decade before the American Revolution, newspapers became increasingly politicized, and in the first generations of the new nation, political factions and parties came to subsidize or sponsor many leading newspapers. Newspaper editors might preach independence but they generally came to practice partisanship. This included editors like the celebrated Horace Greeley. Greeley began his career on a country weekly in the 1830s but moved to New York to run a literary magazine in 1834. In 1840 he ran the Whig campaign paper, the *Log Cabin*, with a circulation up to 80,000 for its brief life, and in 1841 began his own commercial paper, the *New York Tribune*. The *Tribune* was among the first of a new breed of cheap, commercially minded "penny papers" that began to appear in leading cities in the 1830s. This paper, with a circulation of some 10,000 at first, was strongly anti-slavery and clearly showed itself a journal of ideas, reporting on women's rights, socialist experiments, and other topics. Not an advocate of women's rights himself, Greeley nonetheless hired Margaret Fuller in 1844 as the first woman to be a regular staff employee on a major American newspaper. Karl Marx was a European correspondent.

No other newspaper in the country was so cosmopolitan. Few newspapers even dispatched a reporter to the nation's capital. Editors would themselves occasionally visit to do some first-hand commentary but only as politics heated up in the 1850s did newspapers begin to hire Washington reporters, most of whom wrote for half a dozen or more papers and supplemented their salaries with work as clerks for Congressional committees or speechwriters for politicians.[2] The occupational worlds of journalism and politics were not differentiated.

In fact, the metropolitan press at mid-century was practically a subdivision of the political party. Newspapers were fundamental rallying points for political parties. Editors were intimately involved in political patronage. President Andrew Jackson appointed more than 50 journalists to political office; as many as 10 percent of the appointments he made requiring Senate approval were of journalists.[3] A generation later Abraham Lincoln followed suit. He rewarded the editor of the Philadelphia *North American*, a pro-Lincoln paper, with federal appointments and Army promotions for his sons, not to mention substantial federal advertising directed to his paper. Lincoln appointed editors as ministers, first secretaries of missions, or consuls in 15 foreign capitals, and appointed others to customs houses or postmasterships in New Haven, Albany, Harrisburg, Wheeling, Puget Sound, Chicago, Cleveland, St. Louis, and Des Moines.[4] Newspaper work was not an independent calling so much as one path within the political world of the mid nineteenth century.

This partisan press was the press that Alexis de Tocqueville judged both vulgar and irreplaceable for American democracy. He wrote that newspapers were a necessity in a democratic society: "We should underrate their importance if we thought they just guaranteed liberty; they maintain civilization."[5] But Tocqueville complained of the cantankerous outbursts of American journalists.

Tocqueville was impressed by the quantity of American newspapers, as were other European visitors, but he did not understand why there were so many papers scattered across small communities and frontier towns. He took the cause to be the multiple number of responsible governmental units in America. If citizens elected only members of Congress, Tocqueville suggested, there would not be a need for so many newspapers because there would be so few occasions on which people had to act together politically. The multiplication of governmental units in each state and village "compelled" Americans to cooperate with one another, and each one "needs a newspaper to tell him what the others are doing."[6]

In fact, local newspapers in Tocqueville's America told readers very little about what others in their own communities were up to. Most of the papers printed little local news.[7] In the 1820s, when improved mail service brought urban papers more expeditiously to country towns, the country newspapers finally began to run local news in an effort to retain readers with a service the urban papers could not provide.[8] In Kingston, New York, where village government was admittedly a modest affair, the press did not mention local elections in the early 1800s and did not cover village government at all until 1845.[9]

The multiplication of governmental units that caught Tocqueville's eye did afford one thing that helped support the press – government subsidy.

Getting government printing contracts was a great boon to the newspaper. Demand of a democratic audience for news had less to do with the proliferation of newspapers than did the supply of government advertising.

Also important to explaining the large numbers of provincial newspapers was a large supply of would-be editors. Entrepreneurs began newspapers in hundreds of small towns in America not because a population demanded them but because the existence of the paper might attract a population. Country crossroads towns established newspapers, small colleges, and grand hotels, all on the prospect of future growth.[10] The antislavery leaders who founded the town of Emporia, Kansas, in 1857, for instance, began the *Emporia News* within a few months to help create an image of a prosperous community. Nearly all copies of the inaugural issues were mailed East, hoping to attract emigrants to buy town lots and make the fledgling town live up to its public relations efforts.[11] Like the effort to attract the railroads or to win designation as a county seat or site for a state college, the establishment of a newspaper was a tool of real estate development. The character of American newspapers has had something to do with their being advertising-supported media, particularly from the 1830s on, but perhaps owes even more to their being through and through a promotional tool of community and urban development.

The revolt against party in American political culture

Americans today seem to believe that journalists are, or should be, a transmission belt of neutral facts about world events. Their passion should be dispassion. To a remarkable degree, it is. American journalists take pride not in writing pieces of advocacy but in being attacked by both left and right for "writing down the middle."[12] Playing it down the middle became a cherished professional ideal in the United States – and elsewhere, too, but not so thoroughly nor so long ago as in the United States. How did this distinctive brand of American professionalism emerge out of the nineteenth-century partisan press?

What happened was a remarkable transformation of American political culture in the late nineteenth century. In the Progressive era, reformers cleansed voting of what made it corrupt, in their eyes, and compelling, in the eyes of voters. In this Protestant Reformation of American voting, the political party's ability to reward its faithful declined with civil service reform; its ability to punish voters with social disapproval and reward them with coin and drink faded as the privacy of the voting booth grew secure. Even the party's capacity to attract attention declined as commercial forms of popular entertainment begin to offer serious competition. During the era from 1880 to 1920, liberal reformers began to criticize party loyalty. They promoted new forms of electoral campaigning, urging an "educational" campaign with more pamphlets and fewer parades. At the same time, newspapers became more willing to take an independent stance. By 1890, a quarter of daily newspapers in northern states, where the reform movement was most advanced, claimed independence of party. It became common and even respectable for party papers to "bolt" from party-endorsed candidates.

By 1896, a reform known as "the Australian ballot" had swept the country, changing forever the way Americans went to the polls. Until the 1890s, American election days were organized to the last detail by the competing political parties. The parties printed their own tickets and distributed them to voters near the polls. The voter then did not need to mark the ballot in any way – the voter did not need, in fact, to be literate. He just took the ticket from the party worker and deposited it in the ballot box.

The Australian ballot symbolized a different understanding of politics. Now the state prepared a ballot that listed candidates from all contending parties. The voter received the ballot from an election clerk and, in the privacy of the voting booth, marked the ballot, choosing the candidates from one or several parties as he wished. An increasingly strident rhetoric prevailed, condemning the corruption of parties and praising forms of governing that transcended party politics.

Voting, in this new context, was transformed. What had been an act of affiliation became an act of individual autonomy. Where it had been standard practice for parties to convey people to the polls, it was now forbidden in many states. Where party workers had distributed tickets, voters now stood in line to receive their official ballot from state-appointed officials. Where parties had mustered armies of paid election-day workers, many states now outlawed the practice. Where electioneering efforts had accompanied voters right up to the ballot box, new regulations created a moat of silence within so many feet of the polling station.

With the adoption of the Australian ballot, civil service reform, laws forbidding corrupt electoral practices, voter registration laws, forms of direct democracy like the initiative and referendum, the popular primary, the direct election of senators, and non-partisan municipal elections, politics began to be seen as an administrative science that required experts. Voting came to be seen as an activity in which voters make choices among programs and candidates, not one in which they loyally turn out in ritual solidarity to their party. This new understanding of politics helped transform a fiercely partisan press into an institution differentiated from the parties, with journalists more likely to see themselves as writers than as political hangers-on.[13] Turn-of-the-century American reformers succeeded in a more thorough-going set of anti-party reforms than occurred in any other democracy.

This transformation of American political culture was accompanied by an ardent professionalization of journalism. Partisanship endured, but reporters came increasingly to enjoy a culture of their own, independent of political parties. They developed their own mythologies (reveling in their intimacy with the urban underworld), their own clubs and watering holes, and their own professional practices. Interviewing, for instance, had become a common activity for reporters in the late nineteenth century. Earlier, reporters talked with public officials but did not refer to these conversations in print. Politicians and diplomats dropped by the newspaper offices but could feel secure, as one reporter recalled, that their confidences "were regarded as inviolate." President Lincoln often spoke with reporters informally but no reporter ever quoted him directly. Not until the 1880s was the interview a well-accepted and institutionalized "media event," an occasion created by journalists from which they could then craft a story. This new style of journalistic intervention did not erase partisanship but it did presage reporters' new dedication to a sense of craft, and new location in an occupational culture with its own rules, its own rewards, and its own *esprit*.[14]

Interviewing was a practice oriented more to pleasing an audience of news consumers than to parroting a party line. Professionalization and commercialization marched forward hand in hand. Newspapers had become big businesses by the 1880s, with towering downtown buildings, scores of reporters, splashy sponsorship of civic festivals, and pages of advertising from the newly burgeoning department stores. The papers vastly expanded their readership in this growing marketplace; more and more papers counted their circulation in the hundreds of thousands. Accordingly, reporters writing news came to focus on making stories, not on promoting parties. Newspaper circulation leapt forward while the cost of production plummeted with wood pulp as a new source of paper and mechanical typesetting a new labor-saving device. Advertising revenue surpassed subscription fees as the primary source of income as the papers courted new audiences (particularly women). The increasingly commercial orientation of the newspaper certainly helped sustain the innovation of interviewing.

Only after World War I did European reporters adopt the American practice of interviewing – and never so fully as in the United States. In Britain, journalists began to accept the interview after 1900, often through American tutelage. American correspondents, by their example, taught Europeans that their own elites would submit to interviews. The diffusion of interviewing among American journalists seems to have been unaccompanied by any ideological rationale. It fit effortlessly into a journalism already fact-centered and news-centered rather than devoted primarily to political commentary or preoccupied with literary aspirations. It was one of the growing number of practices that identified journalists as a distinct occupational group with distinct patterns of behavior. The growing corporate coherence of that occupational group, generating a demand both for social cohesion and occupational pride, on the one hand, and for internal social control, on the other, would by the 1920s eventuate in a self-conscious ethic of objectivity.

The notion that the move from partisanship to objectivity was economically motivated is widely believed. The leading textbook in the history of American journalism puts it this way: "Offering the appearance of fairness was important to owners and editors trying to gain their share of a growing readership and the resulting advertising revenues."[15] But was it? Readership was growing so rapidly in the late nineteenth century – from 3.5 million daily newspaper readers in 1880 to 33 million in 1920, that a great variety of journalistic styles were economically rewarding. Very likely the most lucrative option remained strident partisanship. Certainly this characterized circulation leaders of the day like William Randolph Hearst's *New York Journal* and Joseph Pulitzer's *New York World*, both enthusiastic supporters of the Democratic Party. Heated political campaigns and the newspapers' ardent participation in them were circulation-builders, not circulation-losers.[16] The devotion of American journalists to fairness or objectivity could not have emerged before journalists as an occupational group developed loyalties more to their audiences and to themselves as an occupational community than to their publishers or their publishers' favored political parties. At this point journalists also came to articulate rules of the journalistic road more often and more consistently. Rules of objectivity enabled editors to keep lowly reporters in check, although they had less control over high-flying foreign correspondents. Objectivity as ideology was a kind of industrial discipline. At the same time, objectivity seemed a natural and progressive ideology for an aspiring occupational group at a moment when science was god, efficiency was cherished, and elites increasingly judged partisanship a vestige of the tribal nineteenth century.[17]

Journalists not only sought to affiliate with the prestige of science, efficiency, and Progressive reform but also sought to disaffiliate from the public relations specialists and propagandists who were suddenly all around them. Journalists had rejected parties only to find their new-found independence besieged by a squadron of information mercenaries available for hire by government, business, politicians, and others. A new "profession" of public relations emerged in and after World War I, churning out press releases, constructing publicity stunts and maneuvering to get favorable attention in the press for their clients. By 1920, journalists and journalism critics complained that there were 1,000 propaganda bureaus in Washington modeled on the war experience.[18] Figures circulating among journalists claimed that 50 percent or 60 percent of stories, even in the *New York Times*, were inspired by press agents. The publicity agent, philosopher John Dewey wrote in 1929, "is perhaps the most significant symbol of our present social life."[19]

Anxious about the manipulability of information in the propaganda age, journalists felt a need to close ranks and assert their collective integrity. By the 1920s, this meant increasingly a scrupulous adherence to scientific ideals. "There is but one kind of unity possible in a world as diverse as ours," Walter Lippmann wrote; "It is unity of method, rather than of aim; the unity of the disciplined experiment." He wanted to upgrade the professional dignity of journalists and provide a training for them "in which the ideal of objective testimony is cardinal."[20] More than a set of craft rules to fend off libel suits or a set of constraints to help editors keep tabs on their underlings, objectivity was finally a moral code.

Some of the sociological conditions that produced these journalistic norms in America were absent or less pronounced in Europe. The desire of journalists to distinguish themselves from public relations practitioners was absent in Europe because public relations developed later and less extensively there. The growing anti-partisan nature of American political culture intensified in the Progressive years and went much farther than efforts to contain party corruption in Europe. In America, a civil service tradition had to be invented and emerged as the result of a political movement; in Europe, a degree of bureaucratic autonomy, legitimacy, and professionalism could be taken for granted, so there was less reason for European civil servants to ideologize themselves the way American reformers did. The ideological virtues of a journalistic divorce from party, so readily portrayed in America against this reform background, had no comparable political ballast in European journalism.

It may also be that the cultural space that could be occupied by objectivity as a professional value in American journalism was already occupied in European journalism. Continental European journalists already understood themselves in a publicly successful way – as high literary creators and cosmopolitan political thinkers. They did not have the down-and-dirty sense of themselves as laborers whose standing in the world required upgrading as American – and British – journalists did. If there was to be upgrading, in any event, it was to a literary rather than professional ideal.

This is much too global a generalization about the many different European journalisms, but there is a good case that it applies very well at least to the French experience. Jean Chalaby has argued that British and American journalism experienced a "unique discursive revolution" and became information and fact-centered in the mid nineteenth century, but French journalism did not. Until late in the century, when leading British and American newspapers employed numerous foreign correspondents, the French press drew most of its foreign news straight from the London papers. The French were much less concerned than the British and Americans about drawing a line between facts and commentary in the news. French journalism was dominated by literary figures and literary aspirations and did not participate in the fact-centered discursive revolution that characterized British and American journalism.[21] The moral norm American journalists live by in their professional lives, that they use as a means of social control and social identity, and that they accept as the most legitimate grounds for attributing praise and blame, is a norm that took root first, and most deeply, in this journalism and not in others across the Atlantic.

The professionalization of American journalism reached a high point in the 1950s and 1960s – what media scholar Daniel Hallin has called its era of "high modernism."[22] In the 1960s and after, criticism emerged inside and outside journalism condemning journalistic professionalism and the norm of objectivity itself as means of catering to established power, particularly governmental authorities. Journalists were judged too polite and too cooperative, too willing to accept Cold War presumptions as their own, too eager to adopt anticommunist ideology and a set of moderate establishment values that took for granted capitalist enterprise, small town virtues, a two-party system, and other values promoted by political elites.[23]

The criticism had consequences. Propelled by the deep rift in establishment politics that the Vietnam war produced, reporters and editors assumed greater authority relative to their own sources. Vietnam, Watergate, the adversary culture of the sixties, the revulsion in the media toward Ronald Reagan's photo opportunities and George Bush's cynically flag-waving victory over Michael Dukakis in 1988 all contributed to a self-consciousness in journalism about both its possibilities and its pitfalls. The practice of journalism has altered significantly, with a more unembarrassed blend of professional detachment, analytic – and hence interpretive – diligence, and market-driven consideration for the passions and interests of the audience than in the immediate past. Yet attachment to a particular vision of journalism – fact-centered, aggressive, energetic, and non-partisan – remains powerful, practically sacred, among American journalists.

The pluses and minuses of the First Amendment

When journalism operates within a liberal democracy, it may operate in a variety of different ways. "Congress shall make no law abridging freedom of speech, or of the press" – this simple, categorical prohibition in the First Amendment (1791) of the US Constitution has been the pride of American journalism. And the pride is not misplaced. The press is more free of government restrictions in the United States than in any other nation on earth. However, the First Amendment does not mean exactly what journalists think it means, nor does it resolve all matters of censorship and constraints on expression. In particular, limits on governmental constraints in the United States have made the American news media more vulnerable to censorship by private media companies themselves than media in countries with strong state trusteeship of an independent media, like Britain, or state-subsidized support for media representing diverse and minority viewpoints, as in the Nordic countries. In the views of a growing number of important critics, following the First Amendment rigidly does not provide the best environment for encouraging freedom of expression. The First Amendment is indeed the bulwark of American press liberty, but whether this is to the greater good of press freedom has become an open question.

Consider Pat Tornillo, who in 1972 ran for a seat in the Florida state legislature. The *Miami Herald* wrote a couple of scathing editorials about him. Tornillo asked for space in the paper to respond, citing a 1913 Florida "right-of-reply" statute that required newspapers to provide comparable space for reply, upon request, when the newspaper assailed the personal character of any candidate for nomination or for election. When the *Miami Herald* refused to satisfy Tornillo's request, he sued. The Florida Supreme Court held that the right-of-reply statute served the "broad societal interest in the free flow of information to the public." Most democracies around the world would agree. Right-of-reply statutes are commonplace.

The *Miami Herald* believed, in contrast, that a right-of-reply statute abridges the freedom of the newspaper to publish what it pleases. The *Herald* appealed the Florida decision to the US Supreme Court. The case posed a classic problem: could government constitutionally enhance public debate and discussion only by staying out of media regulation altogether? Or could it and should it pass press laws not to abridge but to enhance free expression and to make good what the Supreme Court in 1964 in *New York Times* v. *Sullivan* described as "a profound national commitment to the principle that debate on public issues should be uninhibited, robust, and wide-open?"[24]

On the face of it, a right-of-reply statute would seem a boon to public debate, but the US Supreme Court declared otherwise. Chief Justice Warren Burger saw in Florida's statute "the heavy hand of government intrusion" that "would make the government the censor of what people may read and know." For Justice Burger, this is impermissible. If the marketplace is to be the censor, that may be regrettable but it is fully in accord with the Constitution. It is state censorship that the Constitution forbids.

The case here suggests that First Amendment scholar Owen Fiss is correct in referring to the dangers of "managerial censorship" in the American press. Some critics, both European and American, distinguish between "government censorship" and "market censorship," the latter referring to the restrictions of free expression that news organizations submit to in a drive to please consumers, advertisers, and investors to improve profits. But it is more accurate to recognize that the market does not automatically censor anyone or anything; human beings make the decisions to include or exclude expression in the news organizations they control. In the Tornillo case, the market was not directly a consideration at all although, surely, the newspaper managers worried about long-term restrictions on their freedom of operation if the government could mandate certain sorts of publication.[25]

The US Supreme Court, in the Tornillo case, obviously shied away from having the government tell news organizations anything about what they can or cannot, must or must not, provide the public. It has interpreted the First Amendment's prohibition on laws "abridging" the freedom of the press to mean a prohibition on laws "concerning" the freedom of the press.

Obviously, this is a very stringent reading of the role of the government in sustaining a framework for free expression. There is room to disagree about the best legal framework for a democratic media. The US Supreme Court unanimously decided *Tornillo*, but some leading legal scholars think they erred. In their opinion, *Tornillo* fell short of protecting "uninhibited, robust, and wide-open" debate on public issues, the standard Justice William Brennan articulated in the majority opinion in the *Sullivan* decision (1964). The Brennan standard suggests that the First Amendment aims not to protect the individual's autonomy of expression (in practice, the individual news organization's autonomy) but to serve the society-wide goal of rich public debate.

If protecting the autonomy of an individual or an enterprise (a newspaper) enlarges free speech and so enhances public debate, then that autonomy is to be devoutly protected – but not for its own sake. If that autonomy itself interferes with rich public debate, then the state should have legitimate means to intervene to preserve robust debate from individuals or enterprises that might hijack it. By this argument, Pat Tornillo should have won his case.

If the Supreme Court is a trustee and interpreter of "a charter of governance that establishes the institutions of government and the norms, standards, and principles that are to control those institutions," as Owen Fiss writes, then it is vital to keep the large issue of robust public debate in mind.[26] In this view, the protection of the individual autonomy of media institutions against the state is a means, not an end, even if it is a favored means.

This doctrine, of course, opens up a vast array of subtle and difficult decisions. It not only makes clear that current American First Amendment law is revisable but also suggests that very different positions elsewhere may serve democracy as well or better than the liberal-libertarian First Amendment tradition in the United States.

Is the US model a model for anyone else?

The American model cannot be grafted onto any other system. It emerges out of a unique history and it has been shaped by a relationship to distinctive political institutions and a unique political culture. Even as party loyalty and party voting patterns are weakening elsewhere in liberal democracies, the American parties' weakness is extreme. A survey of political consultants worldwide found that 80 percent of Australian consultants judged national party organizations "very important" for candidate electoral success, 64 percent of Western European consultants, 45 percent of Latin American consultants, but only 13 percent of US consultants.[27] Even with the attractions of the First Amendment, other democracies have found alternative ways to establish expressive freedom that involve, rather than avoid, the exercise of national governmental authority.

Other countries will not – nor should they – accept American-style journalism wholesale, even though they may take some lessons from it here and there. What seems to me worth holding up as an ideal in American journalism is the spirit it exhibits at its best. The political theorist Nancy Rosenblum has suggested in a different context that nurturing the values that make democracy work should begin at home and that democracies should learn to cultivate in their citizens a set of virtues that people would manifest in everyday life. She lists two virtues or civic "dispositions" as especially important. The first is what she calls "easy spontaneity," a style of civility in which one treats other people identically and easily, without standing on ceremony. Along with this goes the development of "a thick skin," the disposition to make allowances "and to resist the impulse to magnify slights." Rosenblum's second civic disposition is "speaking up," not in cases of life and death but in the most pedestrian instances of everyday injustice. She calls attention here to the value of a person's making at least a minimum response to ordinary injustice, "an iota of recognition when someone is taken advantage of."[28]

Now, there are other dispositions one might recommend for a democracy – say, taking an appropriate interest in public affairs, or a willingness to listen and to compromise. The two dispositions that Rosenblum calls attention to, however, seem to me very important – and also, unintentionally, very American. Could Mark Twain's famous character Huckleberry Finn be better defined than by "easy spontaneity" and a willingness to "speak up" about injustices, small and large? Huckleberry's virtues may also be the virtues of American journalism at its best. The practice of interviewing politicians that Americans developed and to some degree taught to journalists elsewhere in the world is a perfect institutional manifestation of easy spontaneity. Muckraking or investigative reporting is likewise an institutionalization of "speaking up." Neither is essentially related to boosterism, objectivity, or the First Amendment, although there are some obvious connections. But the spirit of easy spontaneity and the habit of speaking up are features of American journalism worth admiring and, to some degree, they are detachable for export. If they spread beyond US borders, whatever the particular institutional or organizational or cultural apparatus may be in the news practices of other countries, then US journalism makes a contribution beyond American shores.

4

The invention of the American newspaper as popular art, 1890–1930

In 1999, a major traveling exhibit of the paintings of Norman Rockwell was mounted, honoring this enormously popular and famous artist. Rockwell is best known for his more than 300 gentle, sentimental, mildly comic cover illustrations for the mass-market *Saturday Evening Post*, usually portraying some feature of middle American life. But the *New Yorker's* art critic, Peter Schjeldahl, reviewing the exhibit, asserted that Rockwell did not illustrate middle America so much as invent it. Schjeldahl's authority for this claim is that he himself grew up in small towns in North Dakota and Minnesota, just the sorts of places Rockwell supposedly documented in his work. Schjeldahl fished in creeks; he played sandlot baseball. He might have been a boy on a *Saturday Evening Post* cover. Nonetheless, he recognizes nothing of his own childhood in Rockwell's paintings. Rockwell got everything right, he says, "except the confusion that flowed in and through every jot of my own experience." For Rockwell, everything is explained, every visible action has a visible cause. Schjeldahl writes, "The absolute absence of mystery in his art makes me sick." Rockwell is a nineteenth-century positivist "in his bones, convinced that the world is knowable."[1]

Only in Rockwell's paintings, Schjeldahl insists, is this so. Real life is confusion, mystery, sequence without narrative, tellings and re-tellings of the same events, a blooming, buzzing confusion. Art orders it, but only momentarily, a pause button on the flow of things, a sublime hold on the reality of evanescence and incoherence.

Rockwell's paintings, perhaps not very successfully because they strain to repress incoherence rather than face it, hold the flux of human experience at bay. Is this also the task – and the failure – of news? Does the newspaper, in seeking a triumph over incoherence, manage a daily renewal of the human capacity for narrative, coherence, and explanation? Is it a beacon of hope, day after day, providing headlines, weather, sports, stock quotations, cartoons, and recipes unfazed by the horrors of the world even as it reports them? Or do newspapers surpass Rockwell, providing an ingenious representation of our confusions and our struggles? Newspapers are not fine art but they are an industrial art, produced by people trained in art, design, photography, and literature. What kind of literary-artistic objects are they?

Whatever they are, they came in Norman Rockwell's own time to assume their conventional form that has now had a long century's run. Rockwell was born in New York City in 1894, a decade after Joseph Pulitzer moved from St. Louis to Manhattan to inaugurate the modernization of the American press, a year before William Randolph Hearst made his way from San Francisco to New York to create the nation's leading model of sensationalism, and two years before Adolph Ochs migrated from Chattanooga to the same journalistic capital to make the *New York Times* the premier American newspaper of respectability and professionalism. Rockwell grew up at just the time American journalism was itself coming of age. What happened in the world of print between 1890 and 1930 in the United States made of the newspaper a particular cultural style – a museum of the day, a collage of random events, a merger of pictures and words, a cacophony of styles of prose, a townhall of voices, a soapbox of self-promotion, and all of this at the same time.

One observer – of French journalism as it happens, but what he says applies to the American case, too – writes that the newspaper takes miscellaneous items of news, publicity, comment, and information, places them in juxtaposition, and has no ambition that they make sense together. The newspaper thus "instructs us in the apparently irreducible fragmentation of daily experience," and normalizes it.[2] Like the market that at the turn of the century replaced the political party as the foundation stone of the press, the daily paper "is a systematic emptying of any logic of connection." Newspapers "rationalize disjunction; they are organized as disorganization."[3]

If that is the newspaper, it could not be further from Norman Rockwell's insouciance. Rockwell's worlds are complete in themselves. The joke is always internal, no references outside the frame are necessary. The newspaper, in contrast, always points elsewhere. It is always an incomplete rendering of its world, always temporary and destined to be replaced the next day or, in the age of the newspaper website, the next few minutes. Try to read a newspaper in another country, or even another city in one's own country. It is a task that requires considerable effort at translation. You have always arrived in the middle of the story, even if the story is in the end not so very different from the one in your home town. When you are visiting another newspaper, names and places and neighborhoods, flooded with connotation, are opaque. The form, but not much of the content, provides familiarity and comfort.

When the *San Diego Union* announced itself to its readers in the 1890s, it prided itself on containing "the cream of domestic and foreign intelligence, interesting and valuable to every reader." It gave assurance that the paper's policy was "the exclusion from its columns of whatever is offensive to pure thought or aught that would make it objectionable for entering the family circle." The *Union* would seek to "comprehend the actual requirements of all classes" and would render help in "encouraging new enterprises." It would "earnestly watch city, county and state affairs with the utmost jealousy on behalf of the people." Local features, in addition, would help make the paper indispensable: "It will be welcomed to every home, in every counting room, and by every reader as an instructive, pleasant visitor, and a valued friend and advisor."[4]

If the first face of the newspaper is that of barely contained incoherence and incongruity, this is the second face: the friendly visitor. This odd two-sidedness of the newspaper – both discordant and comforting, both a spectacle of the extreme, uncanny, and shocking and a rendering of the familiar – is what gives the institution its peculiar charm (for some) and its irritating smugness (for others).

Insight into the "friendly visitor" side of news came after World War II in a study conducted by Bernard Berelson entitled "What Missing the Newspaper Means." Delivery workers declared a strike against New York's newspapers, shutting down every general daily newspaper in the city. You could go directly to the newspaper office to pick up a paper but you could not have it delivered to your home or find it at one of the city's countless news stands. Mayor Fiorello LaGuardia famously responded to the strike by reading the comics on the radio so that children could keep up with their favorite characters while their voting parents could feel grateful to the mayor.

Berelson interviewed people to find out what, if anything, they missed about not having the news. Some people told him they missed following major stories, but few of them could name an ongoing story they were trying to keep up on. Many complained that it was difficult to follow radio programs without the radio schedule published in the newspapers. Various aspects of everyday living became more difficult without the newspaper. Some people simply missed the activity of reading and substituted for the newspaper anything at hand, especially old magazines lying around the house. People felt uneasy and at a loss: "I like the feeling of being in touch with the world at large. . . . It's like being in jail not to have a paper. . . . I am like a fish out of water, I am lost and nervous. I'm ashamed to admit it." At least half of those interviewed indicated that newspaper reading was part of their daily ritual, something they did, very often, while doing something else – while eating or while traveling to work. Without the newspaper, one person responded, "I sat around in the subway, staring, feeling out of place."[5]

Early American newspapers were not integrated into people's everyday lives in the ways this study suggests. Newspapers circulated primarily among small elites and focused almost exclusively on foreign news, some local commercial information, and advertising oriented to business people and wealthy families more than to ordinary consumers. The newspapers came in a standard format: four pages in length, no illustrations, headline type the same or barely larger than type in the body of the news item. There was no effort at design and, for all practical purposes, no effort at editing. The conductors of the papers simply reprinted whatever came to them from the London papers they gathered up from the latest ships arriving in port. There were no reporters, although friends or acquaintances traveling abroad might send in a letter about what they saw. Colonial newspapers typically showed little ambition for their papers but to advertise their job-printing services and otherwise stay out of trouble by running little or no news of the city in which they published or the colonial province in which they were located.

In the nineteenth century, newspapers became organs of political parties, they circulated more widely, and by the 1820s the more ambitious among them went so far as to move from weekly to daily publication, hiring reporters, including in a few cases Washington correspondents. Still, most newspapers relied heavily on stories reprinted from other papers. Local news remained scarce. In the weeklies of the small towns that dominated the landscape, local news was nearly non-existent. Advertising dominated the look of the press and occupied two or two and a half of the four pages of the paper.

The closeness of the newspapers to the political parties in the mid nineteenth century can scarcely be exaggerated. Still, the bond between party and press would be pried apart by the motive of commerce. Beginning in the 1830s, a new breed of urban paper, the so-called "penny press," discovered that one could make money by printing local news as well as national political news, by hawking newspapers on the street and not selling by subscription only, and by lowering the price of a copy from 6 cents to a penny or two. These innovations attracted readers and readers attracted advertisers. From the 1830s on, but especially in the decades after the Civil War, competition for news grew intense. With competition for readers, with new campaigns and stunts to promote circulation, newspapers developed the sports page, the society page, and other features. Simple language, large headlines, and lavish illustrations became popular and helped extend readership to immigrants and others whose abilities with written English were limited. By 1880, New York City had half a million foreign-born citizens; a decade later, 40 percent of the city's population was foreign-born. Economic changes made a new mass journalism possible, the prospect of profit made it desirable, and the changing habits and inhabitants of the cities made it necessary in the eyes of ambitious publishers.

What would ultimately separate, and, in many cases, sever completely the bond between party and press was, first, the motive of profit as newspaper publishers increasingly found that a consumer market for news interested them more than an audience of partisan fans, and, second, the growing appeal of a political reform movement that questioned the worth of parties altogether. In the 1870s and 1880s, liberal reformers, first among Republicans and then Democrats, began to criticize the very notion of party loyalty. They promoted new forms of political campaigning, urging an educational rather than participatory or "spectacular" campaign, moving from parades to pamphlets, and urging that the exercise of the franchise be understood as the individual citizen's rationally choosing among candidates, parties, and policies rather than demonstrating emotional allegiance to a party label.[6] Newspapers became more willing to take an independent stand. By 1890 a quarter of daily newspapers in the North, where anti-party reforms were most advanced, claimed independence of party. The largest papers were the most likely to be independent.[7]

As late as the 1890s, when a standard Republican paper covered a presidential election, it either deplored and derided Democratic candidates – or simply neglected to mention them. (How much coverage does the Catholic church newsletter provide about the Methodist or Lutheran church across the street? To the extent that the Republican newspaper was speaking to and for a community of the like-minded, attention to rival parties did not feel to the newspaper staff like a professional obligation.) In the days before public opinion polling, the size of partisan rallies was taken as a proxy for likely electoral results. Republican rallies would be described as "monster meetings" while Democratic rallies would often just not be covered at all. For Democratic papers, of course, it was just the reverse.

As indicated in chapter 3, when journalism began to be differentiated from politics, its new independence was besieged by a squadron of information mercenaries available for hire by government, business, politicians, and others. Early in the twentieth century, businessmen and government agencies multiplied their efforts to place flattering stories about themselves in the press. A New York editor complained that the new Pulitzer School of Journalism at Columbia was churning out more "parasites" for the PR industry than reporters.[8]

Journalists felt besieged. One response was to forcefully declare they could not be bought or swayed. The general manager of the Associated Press, Kent Cooper, announced his creed in 1925: "The journalist who deals in facts diligently developed and intelligently presented exalts his profession, and his stories need never be colorless or dull."[9] Newspaper editors formed their own national professional association for the first time in 1922–3, the American Society of Newspaper Editors. At their opening convention, they adopted a Code of Ethics or "Canons of Journalism" that included a principle of "Sincerity, Truthfulness, Accuracy" and another of "Impartiality," the latter including the declaration, "News reports should be free from opinion or bias of any kind."[10]

As journalists grew self-conscious about how manipulable information had become in an age of propaganda, they felt a need to close ranks and to assert their collective integrity in the face of publicity agents' unembarrassed effort to use information (or misinformation) to promote special interests. Joseph Pulitzer, on endowing the School of Journalism at Columbia (in 1904, although classes did not begin until 1913), declared it his ambition to "raise journalism to the rank of a learned profession." By the 1920s, at least some of the more intellectually minded journalists were coming around to his viewpoint and advocating scrupulous adherence to scientific ideals as the hallmark of professionalism.

This is not to say that journalists all grasped this high-minded discipline. A news organization is not the simple product of writers dedicated to the search for truth. It is an endlessly volatile marriage between professional ideals and commercial ones, between the claims of factuality and the claims of story-telling, between the ambitions of analysis and the aims of entertainment. The headline, as editor Harold Evans is said to have remarked, is not an act of journalism but an act of marketing, and there is really very little in the press about which this could not be said. Moreover, the effort to be not only the reporter of news but a friendly visitor has never disappeared from the press. American newspapers not only report conflicts and competitions with professional detachment but also take part in establishing a local community identity. Not infrequently, in the nineteenth century, newspapers were founded in order to draw attention to and increase the real estate values of frontier towns. This "booster" spirit survives and colors the American press. European newspapers, typically national in orientation, with closer ties to national party organizations than to local business elites, are less susceptible to boosterism. But in the central arena of reporting political news, American journalism embraced the objectivity norm and later in the twentieth century promoted it to the wider world.

The American newspaper in the first half of the twentieth century was in its salad days. It prospered with the growth of cities, it prospered with war, it prospered with a growing American interest in the world beyond the nation's own borders. There seemed little it could do except prosper. It was so fundamentally multiform that it could keep adding functions without radically altering its identity as the daily provider of political news. Add the comics. Add the puzzles. Add the horoscopes, the society pages, expand sports coverage, run the radio listings. It was a vehicle of advertising and commerce for local business; a vehicle of ego, ambition, and adventure for its proprietors; a vehicle of intra-urban communication for readers who used its classified advertising columns; an agent of economic development for its home city and region; a medium of urban integration and Americanization for (or against) the immigrants who used it as a primer; an organ of entertainment; an instrument of public health and civic instruction. It could be all these things at once without contradiction.

Amidst all the functions the newspaper performed, including many new ones, its old purpose of political education and political advocacy endured. In the first half of the twentieth century, publishers continued to use their newspaper kingdoms to promote their favored parties, policies, or personal political advancement. William Randolph Hearst ran successfully for Congress in 1902 and 1904, failed in his bid for the Democratic nomination for president in 1904, and ran unsuccessfully for governor in 1906 and mayor (of New York) in 1909, and actively maneuvered and tried to manipulate Democratic Party conventions up to and including 1932.

A landmark year for the publisher–editor in American politics was 1920: in that year both the candidate of the Republican Party and the candidate of the Democratic Party for President of the United States were newspaper men. Warren G. Harding, as is widely known, was the publisher and editor of the town paper of Marion, Ohio. Not so widely recalled is that the Democratic candidate, James M. Cox, at the time Ohio's governor, was the publisher of the *Dayton Daily News*. It was through his career as reporter for, and then owner of, Ohio newspapers that he made his way into politics.[11] But the modes of political advocacy changed, and political advocacy could only be maintained increasingly *sub rosa* and in tension with norms of professionalism. Press and politics have remained intertwined in the twentieth century, even as a professional ethic of nonpartisanship became ascendant.

The publisher's voice migrated to the editorial page. The editorial page survived and continues to endure in every major newspaper in the country. Adolph Ochs is reported to have thought about dispensing with it, when he took over the *New York Times* in 1896, but he did not do so and neither did any of his successors.[12] The Pulitzer Prizes have offered an award for editorial writing from their beginning in 1917. In the 1930s, nearly all newspaper editorial pages endorsed a candidate for president (95 percent). This would decline later, but it was still at 80 percent in 1952.[13] The decline in endorsing at the presidential level may not indicate a reluctance to make endorsements in state and local races. It could be a realistic acknowledgment that the voters are so inundated with information about presidential candidates that the endorsement of the local newspaper means little.

In the 1920s and 1930s, the number of distinctive political voices in newspapers began to multiply as the syndicated political column came into its own. Originating in the 1920s with the work of David Lawrence, Mark Sullivan, Frank Kent, and Heywood Hale Broun, the political column was by the mid-1930s well entrenched. By 1937, Walter Lippmann was syndicated in 155 newspapers, Arthur Brisbane in 180, David Lawrence in 150, and Frank Kent in 125. The *New Republic* observed in 1937 that "much of the influence once attached to the editorial page has passed over to the columnists."[14] Columnists' articles could be selectively dropped, or even altered, by subscribing newspapers, but the columns nonetheless provided a new source of prominent, autonomous voices of authority within the newspaper.[15] Columnists were political actors as well as political commentators. Ernest K. Lindley, a *New York Herald Tribune* columnist, wrote campaign speeches for Roosevelt in 1932, and remained a close friend of the President while covering him in the White House. Of course, Eleanor Roosevelt herself became a columnist in 1935 and her "My Day" column was carried in 140 papers by 1940.[16]

It was in this same period that world events began to more routinely impinge on American life. Ambitious American newspapers began to maintain foreign correspondents, reporters whose independent sphere of activity abroad sometimes provided them a distinctive voice and personal authority. Newspapers between 1880 and 1950 became parlors, with multiple voices and multiple conversations conducted simultaneously. The press sought to maintain its cultural authority in part by sharing it more widely among its contributors – publisher, editor, reporter, columnist, and foreign correspondent.

This was a different mode of political interaction – not the open assertion of partisan loyalties but the use of news space or journalistic access to advance the candidacy, career, or policies of favored politicians without public declaration. Walter Lippmann, the most honored and respected journalist of his day (and his day extended from the 1920s to the 1960s) operated in this fashion. He was not above offering private advice to a favored presidential candidate like Wendell Willkie in 1940. He told

Willkie in July that he would sink his own campaign if he adopted a "1936 mentality" and longed for the pre-New Deal days. Bitterness against the New Deal, Lippmann warned, would position Willkie as a reactionary. (Willkie, as his campaign continued to founder, moved further and further from Lippmann's counsel and Lippmann finally could not support either candidate.) By the way, Wendell Willkie's adultery was well known to journalists covering his presidential campaign; his lover, Irita Van Doren, was literary editor of the *New York Herald Tribune*. Not a word appeared in the press.

In 1940, at the urging of Senator Claude Pepper, Lippmann drafted a plan that became the basis for the Lend-Lease bill. Of course, Lippmann also endorsed Lend-Lease in his newspaper columns. In 1945, Lippmann and *New York Times* writer James Reston convinced the ambitious Republican Senator Arthur Vandenberg that his isolationist leanings would not serve him well if he ever wanted to be President, which he clearly did. The two journalists wrote a speech for Vandenberg that he delivered in the Senate to great acclaim. Reston wrote in the *Times* that the speech was "wise" and "statesmanlike" and Lippmann likewise praised Vandenberg's turn-about in his column.[17]

A good newspaper, playwright Arthur Miller declared, is a nation talking to itself. This is a popular notion among journalists or those who love and celebrate journalism, but it is a metaphor designed to obscure what is unique, useful, powerful, and problematic about the press. No, a good newspaper is not a nation talking to itself. There may be some recognizably human voices in it but, for most of newspaper history, they have tended to be exceptional. Nineteenth-century newspaper prose was normally partisan, extravagant, wordy in the extreme. If that is how nineteenth-century Americans talked to one another, the country was a nation of blowhards. Twentieth-century newspaper prose came to be constrained by a set of conventions of detachment and neutrality, often shaped by circumlocution, often pegged awkwardly to specific events of the preceding twenty-four hours that were poor substitutes for a direct address to the broader issues those events very approximately represented.

So, no, the newspaper is not a nation talking to itself; it is a set of editors and reporters narrating a view of what they understand to be important events to their reader, strained through the peculiar conventions of journalistic culture. It has also been a set of party officials (in the nineteenth century) and public officials (in the twentieth) ventriloquating through the journalists and their newspapers to the public. It has been a set of popular expectations and tastes reflected and inflected through editorial judgment. This is certainly some sort of reflection of the consciousness of a moment but it is "talk" only in a very limited sense. It is intensely and fundamentally visual. If it is talk at all, it is printed talk. More than that, it is planned and designed and organized printed talk. As such, it is an art object. It is a visual representation of the congruences or incongruences of the world, all in one. Newspapers saturated American consciousness in the early twentieth century, in those far-off days when there was no competition with the Internet or television or even, in any large sense, radio. Newspapers were still the cock of the walk, and a man like Hearst, delusional though he was, could realistically imagine himself a president. Walter Lippmann could readily expect presidents to pay him their respects. Walter Winchell could inspire fear in the land from the power of his gossip columns. In the first decades of the twentieth century, the modern newspaper was born, a compendium of competing voices and authorities and genres and styles, a something-for-everyone amusement park, for men and women, young and old, bargain hunters and political junkies and puzzle addicts, investors, and radio fans alike.

We could mourn the loss of the nineteenth century's high seriousness. I don't see why. It was party politics, and party politics then as at present is far from elevating. And it was little else in terms of national news. Little business reporting, little analysis, no reporting on social life and social trends. What these partisan machines became was the modern newspaper, even though our desires for what the newspaper is supposed to be are akin to Norman Rockwell's aspirations for the simple and sentimental world that he brought to the *Saturday Evening Post*. The reality of middle American life was more complex than Rockwell was willing to grasp and the reality of the twentieth-century newspaper more complex and more fascinating than the metaphor of "a nation talking to itself" invites. A new conversation will recognize that print has virtues (and vices) of its own, that it brings gifts to democracy that conversation cannot, and that it is time, in what may be the newspaper's declining life, to assess what it is we have had and what is about to be transfigured.

5

Why democracies need
an unlovable press

Alexis de Tocqueville, widely cited for his view that the American press
is a necessary and vital institution for American democracy, did not actually have much affection for it. He objected to its violence and vulgarity.
He saw it as a virtue of the American system that newspapers were widely
dispersed around the country rather than concentrated in a capital city –
they could do less harm this way. He confessed, "I admit that I do not feel
toward freedom of the press that complete and instantaneous love which
one accords to things by their nature supremely good. I love it more from
considering the evils it prevents than on account of the good it does."[1]

It may well be, taking a leaf from Tocqueville, that today's efforts to
make journalism more serious, more responsible, and, generally speaking,
nicer, are misplaced. I want to propose here that most critics of journalism,
in and outside journalism itself, have attacked just those features of the
press that, for all their defects, best protect robust public discussion and
promote democracy. The focus of the news media on events, rather than
trends and structures; the fixation of the press on conflict whenever and
wherever it erupts; the cynicism of journalists with respect to politics and
politicians; and the alienation of journalists from the communities they
cover make the media hard for people to love but hard for democracies to
do without. These are precisely the features that most regularly enable the
press to maintain a capacity for subverting established power.

This is not to suggest that there is anything wrong with in-depth reporting of the sort that Pulitzer juries and media critics applaud and I greatly
admire. Nor do I mean to suggest that the dialogue of democracy should
jettison editorial writers, Op-Ed columnists, investigative reporters, expert
analysts who can produce gems of explanatory journalism. That would be

absurd. But I do mean to suggest that the power of the press to afflict the comfortable derives more often than not from the journalistic equivalent of ambulance-chasing. Just as the ambulance-chasing trial lawyer sees another person's tragedy as a million-dollar opportunity, the newshound reporter sees it as an attention-grabbing, career-advancing front-page sensation. I want to explore here the ways the most narrow and unlovable features of news may make the most vital of contributions to democracy.

The press as an establishment institution

The press is presumably the bastion of free expression in a democracy, but too often it has been one of the institutions that limits the range of expression, especially expression that is critical of leading centers of power in society. Almost all social scientific study of news shows that journalists themselves, of their own volition, limit the range of opinion present in the news. There are at least three significant ways this happens. First, there is source-dependence. Reporters rely on and reproduce the views of their primary sources and these tend to be high government officials. Second, reporters and editors operate according to a set of professional norms that are themselves constraints on expression. Third, journalists operate within conventional bounds of opinion, opinions common among a largely secular, college-educated upper middle class. All of this has been abundantly documented (and chapter 6 explores the matter more fully). I will quickly summarize the research conclusions but only as a preface to arguing that accounts of the press as unable or unwilling to resist the demands of established political power have been exaggerated.

Dependence on official sources

Media scholars have consistently found that official sources dominate the news. This is invariably presented as a criticism of the media. If the media were to fulfill their democratic role, they would offer a wide variety of opinions and perspectives and would encourage citizens to choose among them in considering public policies. If the media allow politicians to set the public agenda, they may unduly narrow public discussion and so diminish democracy. This is the argument made, for instance, by W. Lance Bennett in his account of the "indexing" function of the press. For Bennett, the media "tend to 'index' the range of voices and viewpoints in both news and editorials according to the range of views expressed in mainstream government debate about a given topic." Bennett argues that this helps perpetuate a "world in which governments are able to define their own publics and where 'democracy' becomes whatever the government ends up doing."[2]

Sociologist Herbert Gans makes an argument about official sources related to Bennett's.[3] For him, the routines of daily journalism undermine democracy. If supporting democracy means encouraging citizens to be active, informed, and critical, then the standard operating procedures of mainstream journalism subvert their own best intentions. Since most news is "top down," relaying the views of high government officials over lower government officials, all government officials over unofficial groups and oppositional groups, and groups of any sort over unorganized citizens, it diminishes the standing and efficacy of individual citizens.[4]

Whether the normative implications of journalism's favoring high government officials are as dire as Gans fears may be doubted, but it is indisputable that news media coverage emphasizes the views and actions of leading politicians and other top government officials. It is likewise indisputable that this limits the range of opinion to which the general public is exposed.

The constraints of professional culture

Journalists favor high government officials – but why? The answer is that they work within a professional culture or a set of professional values that holds that a journalist's obligation is to report government affairs to serve the informational functions that make democracy work. One might still ask why that general function should lead to such a strong emphasis on government officials. The answer seems to be that newspapers, once divorced from direct service to political parties (the leading nineteenth-century model) and once aspiring to neutral or objective professionalism, developed occupational routines and a professional culture that reinforce what media scholar Janet Steele calls an "operational bias" in news reporting. That is, in the work of political reporting, journalists emphasize "players, policies, and predictions of what will happen next." So even when the press goes to outside experts rather than inside government officials, they seek people with experience in government, access to and knowledge of the chief players in government, and a ready willingness to speak in the terms of government officials, interpreting and predicting unfolding events. In television reporting and to a large degree in the print media, too, historians or area experts on the Middle East, for instance, are unlikely to be asked to comment on developments there to set contemporary events in a broader historical and cultural context. It is rare almost to the vanishing point for the press to seek out people even further from the policy-making community to comment on daily political affairs – for instance, religious leaders.[5] The use of religious leaders to discuss key foreign policy matters is essentially non-existent.[6] Why? No publisher dictates that religious opinion is irrelevant. There is no force anywhere dictating anything about this except the well-learned habits and patterns of journalists.

The constraints of conventional wisdom

Journalists seem to be paragons of conventional wisdom. They are wrapped up in daily events, and it would be disconcerting for them and for their readers if they took a long view. It might also be disconcerting for them to take a comparative (non-American) view. It would certainly be disconcerting for them to spend too much time with academics or others removed from the daily fray of political life. It is in relation to the conventional wisdom that journalists know how to identify "a story." Individual journalists may take issue with convention. Some journalists who work for publications with non-conventional audiences may write with unconventional assumptions and unusual points of departure. But the mainstream journalist writing for a standard news institution is likely to be ignorant of, or, if informed, dismissive of opinions outside the fold.

In Washington, in state capitals, and even more in smaller countries, journalists pick up conventional wisdom through lives intertwined with the lives of politicians. In France, for instance, Thomas Ferenczi, associate editor of *Le Monde*, complains that journalists and politicians – and it does not matter if they are left-wing or right-wing – belong to the same "microcosm": "when they are young they go to the same schools, later they live in the same areas, go to the same holiday resorts, and so on." Ferenczi warns, "There is real danger for democracy here: namely, that journalists and politicians, because they are so closely linked, have their own, narrow, idea of what the media should cover . . . and ignore the interests of the people."[7] This is less of a problem in the more pluralistic United States than it is in France. In the United States, there is a more widely dispersed journalistic elite – at least across two cities (New York and Washington) with important pockets of opinion shapers in Los Angeles, Chicago, and elsewhere, rather than concentrated in one – and it is much more diverse in social and educational background. However, the same general phenomenon occurs.

Other factors also limit the range of opinion in the American media, vitally important factors, although they lie outside the news media as such. For instance, the American political system generally offers a narrower political spectrum, and one less accommodating of minorities, than most other democratic systems. Ralph Nader complained bitterly after the 2000 election that he had not been well covered in the press. Why, he asked, when he had been raising real issues did he get no coverage, while Al Gore and George W. Bush, the Tweedle-dum and Tweedle-dee of American politics, got coverage every time they blew their noses? The answer seemed pretty straightforward: Ralph Nader was not going to be elected president of the United States in 2000. Either Al Gore or George W. Bush would. The press – part of its conventional wisdom – believed its job was to follow what the American political system had tossed up for it. It was not the job of the press to offer the public a wide range of issues but to cover, analyze, and discuss the issues the two viable candidates were presenting. Imagine, however, if Ralph Nader had been running for chancellor in Germany. Would the German press have shown greater interest in his ideas? Yes, but not because the German press is better or more democratic, but because Germany has a parliamentary political system. If Ralph Nader's party received 5 percent of the vote in Germany, it would receive 5 percent of the seats in Parliament and Nader would be a force, potentially a decisive force, in forming a government. If Ralph Nader received 5 percent of the vote in the United States, he would get no seats in Congress and would remain an outsider to the legislative process.

So there are many reasons why the media discourse in the United States fails to approximate an ideal of robust and wide open discussion. Even so, journalism as it functions today is still a practice that offends powerful groups, speaks truth to power, and provides access for a diversity of opinion. How and why does this happen despite all that constrains it? The standard sociological analysis of news places it in so airless a box that exceptional journalistic forays are not readily explained. They are the exceptions that prove the rule. They are the ones that got away from the powers of constraint and cooptation and routine. But these "exceptions" happen every year, every week, and at some level every day. How can we explain that?

Strategic opportunities for free expression

Eventfulness

There is a fundamental truth about journalism recognized by all journalists but almost no social scientists: things happen.[8] Not only do things happen but, as the bumper sticker says, shit happens. That is what provides a supply of occurrences for journalists to work with. Shit even happens to the rich and powerful and it makes for a great story when it does.

Because shit happens, journalists gain some freedom from official opinion, professional routines, and conventional wisdom. Journalism is an event-centered discourse, more responsive to accidents and explosions in the external world than to fashions in ideas among cultural elites. The journalists' sense of themselves as street-smart, nose to the ground, adventurers in places where people don't want them has an element of truth to it and it is very much linked to event-centeredness.

News, like bread or sausage, is something people make. Scholars emphasize the manufacturing process. Journalists emphasize the raw material their work brings them to; they insist that their jobs recurrently place them before novel, unprecedented, and unanticipated events. While sociologists observe how this world of surprises is tamed, journalists typically emphasize that the effort at domestication falls short.[9]

The journalists have a point. Sometimes something happens that is not accounted for in any sociology or media studies. Take President Bill Clinton's efforts to create a system of national service. This was part of his 1992 campaign and he mentioned it as one of the priorities of his administration the day after his election. He appointed a friend, Eli Segal, to run a new Office of National Service, and Segal set to work to get appropriate legislation through Congress. The administration's efforts led to passage of the National and Community Service Trust Act that Clinton signed into law in September 1993. One year later, "AmeriCorps" would be officially launched. Segal took charge of orchestrating a major public relations event which would feature President Clinton swearing in 9,000 AmeriCorps volunteers at sixteen sites around the country by satellite hook-up. Every detail was checked, every contingency plan was rehearsed. Segal looked forward to a triumphant day on the South Lawn of the White House followed by extensive, favorable news coverage. At 4.30 a.m. on the morning of the ceremony, Segal's phone rang. The event as planned would have to be scrapped. Why? Because at that hour a deranged pilot crashed his Cessna aircraft into the back of the White House precisely on the spot where the ceremony was to be staged. The news media predictably went gaga over this bizarre and unprecedented event and could scarcely be bothered by the launching of AmeriCorps – no doubt more important than the plane crash, but infinitely more routine.

Social scientists insist that most news is produced by Eli Segals, not deranged pilots. Quantitatively, they are right; the vast majority of daily news items on television or in print come from planned, intentional events, press releases, press conferences, and scheduled interviews.[10] Even so, journalists find their joy and their identity in the adrenalin rush that comes only from deranged pilots, hurricanes, upset victories in baseball or politics, triumphs against all odds, tragedy or reversal in the lap of luxury, and other unplanned and unanticipated scandals, accidents, mishaps, gaffes, embarrassments, and wonders. The scholars delight in revealing how much of the news is produced by the best-laid plans of government officials who maneuver news to their own purposes; the journalists enjoy being first to the scene when the best-laid plans go awry.

On September 13, 1994, the *New York Times'* lead story, and two related stories, covered the plane crash at the White House. Other news was swamped. The story on AmeriCorps ran on page 17. Even there it seemed to be folded into the big story of the day. The third paragraph read:

> Some 850 were inducted as more than 2,000 dignitaries and supporters took part in the ceremony on the North Lawn of the White House. They were kept sweltering there for more than two hours, and an elaborately synchronized satellite television transmission was thrown awry because of the crash of a light plane early this morning on the South Lawn where the event was supposed to have taken place.

Journalists make their own stories but not from materials they have personally selected. Materials are thrust upon them. It can even be argued, as Regina Lawrence has, that in recent years news has become more event-driven and less institution-driven. Moreover, the news media take events not as ends in themselves but as "jumping-off points for thematic exploration of social issues." Content analysis of news over the past 100 years indicates journalists pay increasing attention to context, to reporting events in detail especially when they serve as "invitations for the news media to grapple, however gracefully or clumsily, with political and social issues."[11] This preoccupation with unpredictable events keeps something uncontrollable at the forefront of journalism. The archetypal news story, the kind that makes a career, the sort every reporter longs for, is one that is unroutinized and unrehearsed. It gives journalism its recurrent anarchic potential. And it is built into the very bloodstream of news organizations, it is the circulatory system that keeps the enterprise oxygenated.

The AmeriCorps incident does not show that journalism's passion for events aids democracy; in fact, the story displaced was probably more vital to informing a self-governing public than the story that captured the journalists' attention. But the case still shows that official efforts to play the media can be decisively trumped by startling, unprecedented events. All the media consultants and handlers in the world cannot prevent this – and *that* is what serves democracy, the irresistible drive of journalists to focus on events, including those that powerful forces cannot anticipate and often cannot manage.

Conflict

Almost all journalists relish conflict. Almost all media criticism attacks journalists for emphasizing conflict. But conflict, like events, provides a recurrent resource for embarrassing the powerful.

Consider a story by Randal C. Archibold that appeared in the *New York Times* on January 11, 2003 with the headline: "Nuclear Plant Disaster Plan Is Inadequate, Report Says." To summarize, New York Governor George Pataki had commissioned a report on safety at the Indian Point nuclear power plant just 35 miles away from midtown Manhattan. The report was produced by a consulting group the governor hired, Witt Associates. James Lee Witt, its chief executive, was formerly the director of the Federal Emergency Management Agency. So journalists knew the report was being written, knew its chief author was a high-ranking former federal official, knew roughly when it would appear. This sounds like the kind of government-centered "official" news story critics complain about.

But is it? Why did Governor Pataki commission the report? Clearly, he commissioned it after the September 11 terrorist attack made more urgent the concerns that citizens and citizens' groups had already expressed about the safety of the Indian Point nuclear reactor. The plant's safety became a major local political issue in 2000 when a small leak forced the plant to shut down for nearly a year. So an event – a leak at the plant – spawned political mobilization; lively political mobilization plus September 11, another event, made it necessary for the governor to at least make a show of doing something. September 11 further mobilized opposition to the plant, particularly because one of the hijacked jets flew very close to it en route to the World Trade Center. Governor Pataki finally commissioned the report in August 2002 "in response to the rising outcry over safety at the plant." The Witt Report, whose conclusion could not have been fully anticipated by the governor or anyone else if it was to have legitimacy, declared that the disaster preparedness plan was inadequate for protecting people from unacceptable levels of radiation in case of a release at the plant.

The elected executive of Westchester County, Andrew J. Spano, commented, "the bottom line is the plant shouldn't be here." The reporter made it clear that Witt Associates did not remark on whether the plant should be shut down but, at the same time, noted that the report's view of the emergency plans for the plant "largely reflected complaints voiced for years by opponents of Indian Point."

The Witt Report became news not because the governor's office generated it, but because the governor acted in the face of raging controversy. The continuing controversy made the story news and made the news story interesting. In the end, the report obviously gives legitimacy to the environmentalists and others who had urged that Indian Point be shut down.[12] The news story helped keep opponents of government policy alert, encouraged, and legitimated.

Skepticism about politicians

Political reporters have increasingly made it a point not only to report the statements and actions of leading public officials but to report on the motives behind the actions as well as they can. They report not only the show and the dazzle that the politician wants foregrounded, but the efforts that go into the show and the calculations behind them. They do not intend to undercut the politicians, but they do intend not to be manipulated. The result is a portrait of politicians as self-interested, cynically manipulative, and contemptuous of the general public.

Take, for instance, the *New York Times'* April 16, 2003 front-page story on the proposed Bush tax cut, "In a Concession, Bush Lowers Goal of Tax Cut Plan." The story began curtly observing that President Bush lowered his target for a tax cut in a tacit admission that his original package was "dead." Then reporter Elisabeth Bumiller cites White House advisers who said "that they were now on a war footing with Capitol Hill" to pass the biggest tax cut they could. They, along with other Republican strategists, said "it was imperative for Mr. Bush to be seen as fighting hard for the economy to avoid the fate of his father, who lost the White House after his victory in the 1991 Persian Gulf war in large part because voters viewed him as disengaged from domestic concerns." The orientation of the story was to the timing and style of the president's speech on the economy, not to its substance. The background – strategy and image – is the foreground. This kind of a story, once exceptional, has become standard.[13]

At the end of September 2003, Laura Bush went to Paris as part of the ceremonies signaling the American re-entry to UNESCO after a boycott of nearly two decades. The First Lady's trip was, of course, a well-planned public relations gesture. Would anyone have suspected otherwise? But Elaine Sciolino, the *Times'* veteran foreign correspondent and chief Paris correspondent, made a point of it, noting that Mrs. Bush did not face the American flag as the American national anthem was sung: "Instead, she stood perpendicular to it, enabling photographers to capture her in profile, with the flag and the Eiffel Tower behind. The scene was carefully planned for days by a White House advance team, much to the amusement of longtime UNESCO employees."[14]

Reporting of this sort – showing the president or in this case his wife as performers putting on their makeup – is a sign of a free press. A particularly dramatic example was the decision of *Time* magazine to run, as its October 6, 2003 cover, the carefully staged and widely celebrated photograph of President Bush, attired in a flight jacket and standing on the deck of an aircraft carrier in early May. Behind the president was the much-discussed banner that boldly proclaimed, "Mission Accomplished," signaling the victorious end of the Iraq war. But the prematurely declared end of the war unraveled in the next months and now the magazine provided its own emphatic headline: "MISSION NOT ACCOMPLISHED."

This kind of reporting may not be a sign of a press that motivates or mobilizes or turns people into good citizens. It may do more to reinforce political apathy than to refurbish political will. But it may be just what democracy requires.

Outsider news

Why was Trent Lott forced out of his post as majority leader of the US Senate? The answer is that, on December 5, 2002, he made remarks at Senator Strom Thurmond's 100th birthday party that suggested Americans would all be better off if Senator Thurmond, running on a segregationist platform for the presidency in 1948, had won the election. The room apparently was full of politicians and journalists, none of whom immediately caught the significance of the remark. It was all part of the general celebration of the extraordinary event of a 100th birthday party for the man who had served in the Senate longer than any other person in American history. No one objected to or even noticed the over-the-top encomium that could at best have been interpreted as thoughtless but, if it was judged to have any real content at all, would have to have been viewed as racist.

But if no one noticed, how did it become news and force Lott's resignation from his leadership post?

The first part of the answer is that several practitioners of the still novel "blogs," personal websites that serve as a kind of highly individualized public diary, took note of Lott's remarks, including several prominent and widely read bloggers. These included Joshua Marshall (at talkingpointsmemo.com), Timothy Noah (at slate.com), and Andrew Sullivan (at AndrewSullivan.com) – all three of them journalists. Noah and Sullivan were once employed by (and in Sullivan's case served as editor of) the *New Republic*. Marshall had worked for the *American Prospect*. Although mainstream press outlets, both print and broadcast, noted the remarks (and C-SPAN had aired them), the bloggers pressed the fact that Thurmond ran as a segregationist and that Lott had taken many conservative stands through the years, including speaking before white supremacist groups and voting against the Civil Rights Act of 1990. Matt Drudge, in his on-line report, even found that Senator Lott had made an almost identical statement in praise of Thurmond in 1980.

Thanks to the "blogosphere," the party that Senator Lott and nearly everyone else present regarded as an insider event was available for outsider news. Moreover, as Heather Gorgura argues, the bloggers succeeded in getting the "dump Lott" bandwagon moving not simply by pointing out an indiscreet remark but, in documenting Senator Lott's long and consistent history of association with organizations and policies offensive to African-Americans, by persuading mainstream journalists that Lott's remarks were not casual and thoughtless but representative of a racism Lott had repeatedly expressed and acted upon.[15]

The bloggers do not yet have an economic base.[16] Those with apparently the greatest influence are those who either are, or were recently, journalists for standard news publications. In 2003, the California gubernatorial recall race attracted national blogospherean controversy when Dan Weintraub, a political reporter for the *Sacramento Bee*, roused the ire of Latinos at his paper and beyond for remarks on his own Weblog critical of Lieutenant Governor Cruz Bustamante. His newspaper decided that blogs by its reporters should be submitted to editing – but most journalists and other free speech advocates around the country were horrified by that policy.[17]

The cyber-pamphleteers today can attract broad attention, including the attention of the old media. They do so, I might point out, by name-calling sensationalism. The most prominent and most consequential cases are those of Matt Drudge breaking the Monica Lewinsky story – "The President is an adulterer" – and the bloggers who cried, "The Senator is a racist." An unlovable press, indeed, but perhaps just what democracy requires.

Outsiders are always troublemakers. The news media are supposed to be institutionalized outsiders even though they have in fact become institutionalized insiders. There is much more that might be done to keep journalists at arm's length from their sources. This is something that journalism education could orient itself to more conscientiously – for instance, insisting that journalism students take a course in comparative politics or a course on the politics and culture of some society besides the United States. A serious US history course would also help. The idea would be to disorient rather than orient the prospective journalist. Disorientation – and ultimately alienation of journalists – helps the press to be free.

Social scientists regularly observe how much reporters have become insiders, socializing with their sources, flattered by their intimacy with the rich and powerful, dependent on intimacy for the leaks and leads officialdom can provide. All of this is true, but it is all the more reason to observe carefully and nurture those ways in which journalists remain outsiders.

Bloggers, in the Trent Lott case, although journalists, took up outposts on journalism's frontier, outside conventional news organizations. But even standard-issue journalists are outsiders to the conventional opinions of government officials in several respects. For one, they advance the journalistic agenda of finding something novel that will set tongues a-flutter across a million living rooms, breakfast tables, bars, lunch rooms, and lines at Starbucks. Second, journalists have access to and professional interest in non-official sources of news. Most important of these non-official sources is public opinion as measured by polls or by informal journalistic "taking of the pulse" of public opinion. The American press in particular has a populist streak that inclines it toward a sampling of civilian views. A front page story in the April 24, 2003 *Chicago Tribune*, for instance, by Jill Zuckman, the *Tribune's* chief Congressional correspondent, and date-lined Northfield, Wisconsin, was based on both national opinion polls and local interviewing of people who objected to the USA Patriot Act. The story piggybacked on the frequent informal sessions Wisconsin Senator Russ Feingold held with his constituents. Feingold, not incidentally, was the only Senator to have voted against the Patriot Act.

Zuckman wanted, as she says, "to take the pulse of the voters," especially on the war in Iraq, and she thought that she would be able to sample the widest range of opinions if she traveled with a Democratic Senator during the spring recess. She ended up with Senator Feingold when she learned that he holds town meetings almost every recess and weekend in fulfillment of a campaign pledge to visit every county in the state. As it happened, the Iraq war was declared over before the town meetings began, and people had little to say about the war – but they had a surprising amount to say about their fears for domestic civil liberties. So the topic Zuckman wrote about was not what she intended to cover, but her populist instinct made it possible to report on a phenomenon that elites did not anticipate and that the administration could not have found comforting.[18]

Conclusion

Journalists are not free agents. They are constrained by a set of complex institutional relations that lead them to reproduce day after day the opinions and views of establishment figures, especially high government officials. They are constrained by broad conventional wisdom that they are not well placed to buck and they are powerfully constrained by the conventions and routines of their own professionalism. At the same time, they are not without some resources for expanding the range of expression in the news. What are the structures that can preserve their capacity to speak freely themselves and to expand the range of voices and views they represent in their reporting? What journalistic predispositions can enable them to take advantage of their limited but real autonomy to fulfill the potential of a free press for vigorous, robust discussion of public issues? I am defending, somewhat to my surprise, what are usually attacked as the worst features of the American press – a preoccupation with events, a morbid sports-minded fascination with gladiatorial combat, a deep, anti-political cynicism, and a strong alienation of journalists from the communities they cover.

I hasten to add that the journalists I most admire get behind and beneath events, illuminate trends and structures and moods and not just conflicts, believe in the virtues and values of political life and the hopes it inspires, and feel connected and committed to their communities – global, national, or local. The journalists of greatest imagination discover the non-events that conceal their drama so well. They recognize the story in conflicts that never arose because of strong leadership or a stroke of luck, or the conflict that was resolved peacefully over a painstakingly long time without sparking a front-page "event." But I propose, nonetheless, that some of the greatest service the media provide for democracy lies in characteristics that few people regard as very nice or ennobling about the press. These features of journalism – and perhaps these features more than others – make news a valuable force in a democratic society, and this means that – if all goes well – we are saddled with a necessary institution we are not likely ever to love.

6

The concept of politics in contemporary US journalism

Journalists cover politics. The most important journalists are the ones most likely to be on a political beat, most likely to cover front-page news, and most likely to associate with the most powerful and respectable news sources. Politics is at the summit of what journalists and the broader culture count as our public and noteworthy common life.

But what is politics? What counts as politics in the American press? What topics migrate in, or out, of the political? It is clear, for instance, that various "women's issues," like public facilities for battered women or maternity leave policies or funding for child care centers, are today part of what counts as politics where they were not before the 1970s. This has very little to do with journalism and very much to do with what the world beyond journalism offers up to it. The women's movement changed what counts as politics for both politicians and journalists. Still, journalists do not mechanically record a transparent political scene. They filter the world through a set of preconceptions about what politics is and should be. What are their preconceptions? What presuppositions about politics shape political coverage and provide an orientation to it?

To my mind, the best general account we have of US journalists' intellectual baggage concerning politics is sociologist Herbert Gans' characterization of American journalism as "Progressive" in his classic study *Deciding What's News*. Gans came to his view based on fieldwork at the *CBS Evening News*, the *NBC Nightly News*, *Time*, and *Newsweek* in 1965–9, with updates in 1975 and 1978. When he called American journalism "Progressive," he meant that it tends to share a view of politics most fully elaborated among reformers of the Progressive Era of the late nineteenth and early twentieth centuries. News as mainstream American journalists produce it "is not so much conservative or liberal as it is reformist" and the values it presumes and purveys are "very much like the values of the Progressive movement of the early twentieth century."[1]

Gans observes that domestic political news focuses on corruption, conflict, protest, and bureaucratic malfunctioning that lead government to deviate from "an unstated ideal." He labels that ideal "altruistic democracy" and argues that the nature of news in the American press "implies that politics should follow a course based on the public interest and public service."[2] This broad framework leads him to specify several propositions about the concept of politics in American journalism that serve well, almost thirty years later, to characterize journalistic political values. I extract these propositions from *Deciding What's News*, although they are not listed there in this form. As such, this chapter is a kind of long footnote to Gans, making more explicit some of the implications of his work (although there is no presumption that Gans would agree with everything I am claiming).

The key propositions I will discuss are the following:

1. Politics can be understood as a contest with "winners and losers more than heroes and villains."[3]
2. Politicians should be "honest, efficient, and dedicated to acting in the public interest."[4]
3. Politicians and democracy should be meritocratic; thus civil service appointees are preferred to political appointees and both are held to a standard of efficiency – while waste and red tape should be decried or ridiculed.
4. Citizens should participate: "'Grass roots activity' is one of the most complimentary terms in the vocabulary of the news."[5]
5. It is acceptable and desirable to endorse "the official norms of the American polity," largely drawn from the Constitution.[6]
6. Politicians and citizens should practice moderation in politics.[7]
7. Politics should be represented in a way different from the portrayal of economics. Journalists should regularly report political and legal failures to achieve "altruistic and official democracy" but need not be greatly concerned with "economic barriers that obstruct the realization of the ideal."[8]

I will take up each of these propositions in turn.

Proposition 1.   Politics is a contest

Politics is portrayed in the US press as a war or battle between the President and those who would seek to embarrass him, unseat him, or defeat him at the polls. Consider the lead story in the *New York Times* of June 15, 2001.[9] Lizette Alvarez, reporting from Washington, wrote a story under the headline "Senate Passes Bill for Annual Tests in Public Schools." Her lead was: "In a victory for President Bush, the Senate today overwhelmingly passed a bill to require annual school testing and penalize failing schools if they do not improve." Now, this was also a victory for the "standards" movement in education that had been gathering steam for more than a decade. It may or may not have been a victory for children in schools or for the cause of improving education. But "victory for Bush" was the chief focus of the story: "In the end, the Senate handed President Bush a legislative triumph on an issue he heavily promoted on the campaign trail and hoped to turn into a chief accomplishment of his first year in office." The time frame that serves this article is the four-year first term of the Bush administration. Clearly, President Bush had an interest in gaining a notable "accomplishment of his first year" to burnish his reputation as an effective president, whether or not the legislation eventually improved education. For Alvarez and her editors, the political context, which can be observed in the moment, and not the policy outcome, which is a matter of speculation and which could only be evaluated a year or more later when the new policy began to have impact, is the acceptable focus of Washington reporting. In the seventh paragraph, Alvarez observes that "some analysts" predicted that the legislation would have little impact on education. Two of those analysts, mentioned by name, appear in paragraphs 29 through 32 of a 32-paragraph story.

There is nothing special about the *New York Times* here. The Associated Press story as printed in the *San Diego Union-Tribune* began, "In a triumph for President Bush, the Senate overwhelmingly passed ground-breaking education legislation yesterday that requires annual math and reading tests for millions of schoolchildren as part of an effort to improve the nation's public schools."[10] This 24-paragraph story focuses exclusively on the politics of passing the legislation. It makes no reference at all to the likely impact of the bill on schools or children.

Politics, in short, is a contest with winners and losers. Politicians desire election and re-election, chained to a hormonal cycle that varies with proximity to the sequence of national elections that by law take place on the first Tuesday after the first Monday in November in even-numbered years. The emphasis on politics as a contest over office rather than a contest over policy may have as much to do with journalists' view of journalism as with their view of politics. This, too, is a product of the Progressive Era. As newspapers became free-standing commercial entities, independent of party subsidies, as they increasingly competed to get "the story" faster and more fully than rivals and came to take it for granted that there was a single factual story to get, and as they grew into large organizations with a corps of reporters who developed their own occupational norms and practices disconnected from partisan politics, journalists found meaning and pride in independence and professionalism.[11]

Proposition 2.   Politicians should serve the public interest

Politicians should be honest, efficient, and dedicated to the public good. How could anyone disagree? Would anyone advocate that politicians act dishonestly? No, of course not, but some conscientious political analysts would certainly praise politicians who act for their party, their constituency, or their own re-election prospects as earnestly as they represent the "public interest." US political journalism, in contrast, typically disapproves of political work that is parochial in any of these ways.

Take the case of politicians who act out of loyalty to their party. Political parties exist to win elections, not to serve the public interest. Winning elections is their only reason for being. Journalists therefore find political parties and partisanship contemptible, the most bloated and empty versions of "special interests." The only notable exception to this is that journalists sometimes view parties nostalgically. Columnist Andrew Sullivan wrote thoughtfully on this score when he noticed, at the end of May, 2001, that, in the same week that Senator Jim Jeffords of Vermont was lionized in the press for showing independence of mind and breaking from the Republican Party, Joe Moakley, a long-time Democratic Congressman from Massachusetts who had just died, was eulogized as a Democratic Party loyalist. "As soon as we're born," Moakley had said in 1989 of his own political culture, "we're baptized into the Catholic Church, we're sworn into the Democratic Party, and we're given union cards." Moakley took his role as Congressman to be that of "funneling vast quantities of other Americans' money into local projects that rewarded local supporters." For the support he got from the party for these efforts, he repaid it "with unremitting docility." Jeffords, who routinely voted against the majority in his party, was "the anti-Moakley. And while Moakley benefited from being a plain-talking patronage pol, Jeffords burnished his craggy fickleness as the perfect expression of the quirky state he represented. It paid off in the media."[12]

The media loved Jeffords for a few exciting weeks. Why? Not because journalists are Democrats, although, in the most powerful national news outlets, most are. But the media have also lionized Senator John McCain, a staunch Republican, and for the same reasons they liked turncoat Republican Jeffords – they admire craggy independence. For the journalists, the only good party hack is, like Moakley, a dead one.

If partisanship is contemptible to American journalists, personal political ambition is even worse. The satirical weekly, the *Onion*, got this just right in a mock headline: "Critics Accuse Joe Biden Of Running For President For Political Reasons." The story went on to quote Biden's critics as saying that his ambitions "include exercising veto power over Congress, appointing Supreme Court justices, and even assuming the rank of commander-in-chief of our armed forces if it means he can exert his will over national policy."[13]

Proposition 3.   Politicians and democracy should be meritocratic

Government should be meritocratic, rational, and efficient. That civil service appointees should be preferred to political appointees and that waste and red tape are the iatrogenic diseases of big government are ideas so pervasive in American political culture as to be invisible. But they are not neutral views. Again, they stem from an anti-party position, quintessentially Progressive. Civil service reformers were intensely moralistic, the leaders "as evangelical (and as strenuously resisted) as any crusaders in history."[14] One reformer, George William Curtis, predicted that the first administration to champion the civil service cause would "acquire a glory only less than that of the salvation of a free Union."[15]

Even more sacred than non-partisanship in office is independence from lobbyists or special interests. Elected and appointed officials should not be bought or even swayed by association with powerful interests. They should not serve themselves at the public's expense but nor should they be the puppets of other individuals or groups who seek unfair advantage. This is a routine topic of political scandal. The *San Diego Union-Tribune* and Copley News Service won a Pulitzer Prize in 2006 for exposing the bribes that induced San Diego Congressman Randy "Duke" Cunningham to seek favors for the defense contractors who showered him with cash. When a former lobbyist for farmers in California's Central Valley became a deputy assistant secretary for water and science in the Bush administration's Interior Department, charged with reviewing requests from the very water users' association that had recently employed him, it occasioned a front-page story in the *New York Times* detailing apparent conflicts of interest of a number of Interior Department officials.[16]

Proposition 4.   Citizens should participate

Citizens should participate and, like politicians themselves, should do so
with the public good in mind. The ideal model, as Gans suggests, is the
rural town meeting – "or rather . . . a romanticized version of it."[17] Unself-
ish participation by the masses is good but lobbying and pressure on behalf
of individual or group self-interest is suspect. Every election brings with
it local news stories that celebrate the act of voting and editorials from
both liberal and conservative opinion pages urging citizens to vote, praising get-out-the-vote efforts and, in the aftermath of the election, bemoan-
ing low turnout. The limit to this praise of grass roots activity is that it
should be civil and orderly and linked to conventional electoral politics.
Protest politics, rather than mass actions that are oriented to electoral politics, may be viewed skeptically or derisively.[18]

Proposition 5.   The official norms of
American government are good

Journalists take it for granted that the official norms of American government, identified primarily in the Constitution, are good, or even, among
the nations of the world, exemplary. Violations of these norms are news –
though some norms more than others; challenges to freedom of the press
and related civil liberties regularly make news, although violations of
the civil liberties of radicals or due process for criminals "are less newsworthy."[19] Are the detainees at Guantanamo "out of sight, out of mind?"
To some extent, they are. But the norms of journalism run against this. The
most insistently non-partisan of all American news organizations – the
Associated Press – was responsible for filing the Freedom of Information
Act request that in early 2006 led to the release of thousands of pages of
information about many of the Guantanamo detainees.[20]

Proposition 6.   Americans should
practice moderation in all political things

The journalistic focus on the official norms of the Constitution, like its
praise of citizen participation, has limits. Journalists who found much to
applaud in the civil rights movement also found much to criticize when
the movement's insistence on gaining Constitutional rights seemed "impatient." When assaults on the barriers to voting rights and to equal treatment

in public accommodations, even though entirely in accord with Constitutional guarantees, threatened to provoke violent resistance, liberal opinion
in the press backed away. Martin Luther King, Jr., has become sanctified
with the passage of time as a consensus American hero, but as he was
desperately trying to hold the civil rights movement together in the early
1960s, liberal northern newspapers, like liberal clergy who had given him
support, criticized him for sponsoring protests that might provoke violent
reactions, for relying too much on mass demonstrations and not enough
on less confrontational legal proceedings, and for simply pushing too
quickly to attain long-denied Constitutional rights.

Proposition 7. Politics and the marketplace are separate realms

The news radically separates politics from economics; it regularly reports
political and legal failures to achieve "altruistic and official democracy"
but "it concerns itself much less with the economic barriers that obstruct
the realization of the ideal."[21] Identifying this as a proposition of American
journalism, Gans offers a social democratic critique of liberalism. His
position does not sufficiently recognize the strong tendency of reporters to
cover the impact of "special interests" on the political process. In fact,
journalists are deeply suspicious of the impact of concentrated wealth on
politics, so much so that they have consistently exaggerated the role of
campaign contributions in US elections.[22] Of course, it was only with
campaign finance disclosure requirements that became law in the 1970s
that reporters had the tools available to cover campaign contributions. On
the whole, Gans' proposition is still true and journalism pays deference to
private enterprise – but not when the topic is the direct influence of economic organizations on political decision-making.

A local news story gives a sense of this reflex in US political reporting.
Before San Diego's March 5, 2002, primary election, a controversy raged
over whether alcoholic beverages should be banned on the local beaches.
There was a lot of great stuff here for news hounds – a battle between the
old and the young, between domestic tranquility and liberty of action,
between city hall business as usual and grass roots activism. In early
reporting, a lot of these conflicts began to come out – but then they all
dried up when the leading local daily, the *San Diego Union-Tribune*,
accepted the Watergate adage to "follow the money." The reporter found
– surprise! surprise! – that liquor interests were financing the effort to
defeat the alcohol ban. This was offered as an exposé – "The campaign
against a round-the-clock trial ban on drinking alcohol at two San Diego

beaches was funded largely by alcohol-related businesses, financial documents show."[23] That was the end of the story; at that point most coverage resolved itself into the grass roots good guys versus the special interest, alcohol-soaked, money-grubbing, special-interest bad guys. There was no longer a need to consider whether alcohol bans worked in other communities, or how serious the problem really was, or whether alcohol abuse in the relevant communities really stemmed from beach use of alcohol or from the commercial areas of bars and restaurants adjacent to the beaches.[24] Campaign contribution data easily displaced other discussion because journalists' news values include a distaste for lobbyists and special interests. As Gans declared, "organized lobbying on behalf of citizens' interest is still reported in suspect tones."[25]

Are journalists Progressives or cynics?

Where Gans in 1979 saw Progressivism, others writing years later see cynicism. "The real bias of the press today," writes Thomas Patterson in an extensive content analysis of twenty years of American political reporting:

> is not a partisan one, but a pronounced tendency to report what is wrong with politics and politicians rather than what is right. This type of reporting passes for watchdog journalism but is nearly ideological in its premise: most politicians are presumed to be incompetent, venal, or deceptive, and it is the journalists' role to let everyone know that's the way it is.[26]

Patterson may overstate his case, but it is easy to find examples to support his view. Take the story in the *New York Times* in June, 2001, on the anniversary of D-Day. President Bush went to Bedford, Virginia, a small town that lost 19 of its young men in the first 15 minutes of battle in the D-Day invasion. In Bedford, he dedicated the National D-Day Memorial, a dramatic set of granite sculptures. All of this is faithfully reported in the first eight paragraphs. The ninth paragraph goes directly to President Bush's speech, quoting from it. The tenth paragraph then seeks to set in perspective not the D-Day anniversary but the President's use of it:

> Mr. Bush uses such appearances – and they are frequent these days – to remind voters of his commitment to supporting the United States military. In the past few weeks, he has spoken at the Navy graduation at Annapolis, Md., attended Memorial Day events in Washington and Arizona, and visited Camp Pendleton, Calif. He clearly enjoys military crowds, who often cheer him wildly.[27]

What the explanatory paragraph does, from one point of view, is to undercut the dignity of the President's visit and the sincerity of his speech by outlining its political motives. True, the reporter shows deference to the President by framing the story as Mr. Bush and his aides intended. He introduces his own political expertise only ten paragraphs down, demonstrating to readers that he can read the President's self-interested motives. In adding this political context, the reporter manifests a suspicion of all but altruistic motives.

The question is not whether it is right or wrong to add a "political context" to the bare facts of the story. The question is: what do journalists assume a political context *is*? The answer remains the one that Gans provides: a political context is a political contest. Since a political contest pits one self-interest against another self-interest, and since all self-interest violates the norms of altruistic democracy, political news delegitimates political activity.

Take another example of how this undercutting operates. On Martin Luther King Day in 2002, President Bush received Coretta Scott King at the White House and accepted from her a portrait of Martin Luther King, Jr., to be displayed in the White House. Then the reporter remarks, in the second paragraph, that the presentation took place in the East Room, where Dr. King had once stood to witness President Johnson's signing of the Civil Rights Act. In the holiday ceremony, Mr. Bush "used the opportunity to invite many black leaders to the White House, the kind of event that was commonplace during the Clinton administration." Surely this is an implied criticism of President Bush. One Democratic President offered blacks substance, another offered them at least social inclusion, and this (Republican) President has offered them nothing at all. This is spelled out in the next sentence: "But Mr. Bush, who received less than 10 percent of the black vote in the 2000 election, has often struggled to find ways to reach out to black leaders."[28] No good deed, it seems, is likely to go unpunished by the media when it is performed by a politician, any politician, whose motives are almost exclusively electoral, who is surrounded by "handlers" and pollsters who calculate even transitory symbolic gestures.

When President Bush spoke of how his mother-in-law had lost money in the Enron collapse, the press treated this almost at once as suspect. "To listen to President Bush, it was almost as if an epiphany involving his mother-in-law drove him to turn on the Enron Corporation, his most generous political benefactor," was Richard L. Berke's *New York Times* lead. And then the next paragraph: "But people close to Mr. Bush said his mother-in-law, Jenna Welch, served as a convenient device for him to distance himself from the Enron debacle and to appear more empathetic to its investors and employees than to the wealthy business executives who escaped the Enron collapse with flush bank accounts." The next paragraphs cite White House officials who "insisted" that this was not a strategic decision on President Bush's part but simply repeated in public, in response to a reporter's question, what the president had been saying privately for weeks. Still, Berke continued, other unnamed White House aides assured him that the President's remarks came after Karen P. Hughes and other aides urged him to distance himself more aggressively from Enron.[29]

These instances notwithstanding, Gans' characterization of journalism as "Progressive" seems to me closer to the truth than Patterson's estimation that journalists are "cynical," even if the results are consistent with both the naïve optimism of Progressive values and the weary cynicism Patterson detects. Some of the negative reports today about politics and politicians reflect a growing skill among leading news organizations in living up to a Progressive ideal, not a growing sense that politicians are never to be trusted or that politics cannot be a source of hope. The line between a "Progressive" suspicion of party politics and an apolitical cynicism about politics altogether is not easy to draw and I do not know of evidence to confirm my judgment that Gans is closer to the crux of the matter than Patterson. It just makes more sense, I think, to attribute a widely distributed feature of American journalism to a widely shared cultural understanding of politics, rooted in the rise of independent journalism in the Progressive Era, rather than to faults of personality or flaws of character among journalists that the charge of "cynicism" suggests. And – this is an entirely subjective impression – political journalists I know seem deeply interested in politics and sometimes even in public policy, their skepticism conforming more to the comic definition of a pessimist as "an optimist who has been mugged" than to a deeper cynicism.

Alternatives to Progressive political assumptions

What's wrong or, if not wrong, at least partial or limited about a Progressive Era model of politics?

If that question is to be answered, there must be alternative views of politics consistent with democratic government. There are, and not only in, say, European politics where political parties have represented more ideologically coherent positions and so have not been as susceptible to the criticism that they are wholly opportunistic vote-getting machines. There have been alternative visions of politics in the American experience, too.

In the world of colonial Virginia where Washington and Jefferson grew up and learned their politics, the job of the voter – that is, the white male owning property – was to do no more than affirm the right to rule of the solid citizens of his community. The actual practice of voting in colonial Virginia made this clear. There were no parties. There were no nominations. Leading landowners talked among themselves and figured out whose obligation it was to stand for office each time. If there was more than one candidate, the two candidates would stand by the sheriff who supervised the polling place. A voter approached the sheriff and would say his vote out loud in the presence of the candidates and the other voters. He would then step over to the candidate he had just voted for, shake his hand, and so confirm a social relationship within an established hierarchy.

In such a world, citizens' obligation was to turn back the ambitious and self-seeking at the polls. But they were not encouraged to evaluate public issues themselves. That was what representatives were for. Not parties, not interest groups, not newspapers, not the citizens in the streets, but legislatures and legislatures alone would deliberate and decide.

The founders' "good citizen" was not the same as ours. The good citizen at our nation's founding was a deferential citizen, someone who knew his place. The "grass roots" were suspect, not an object of adulation. For most of the nineteenth century, in contrast, organized parties dominated the political scene. The informational demands on citizens in this partisan era remained minimal but the demands for fraternity were large. Take voting – the voter did not even have to mark a ballot. He picked up a ticket from a party worker at the polls, a so-called "ticket peddler." He did not mark it. He did not even have to look at it. He just put it in the ballot box. Literacy was not required; indeed, legal citizenship was not required in many states. Political activity did not demand knowledge of the issues but convivial and ritual participation in barbecues, torchlight processions, pole raisings, parades, and festivals. Politics was a business of solidarity. It was composed of intense, open rivalries that, more often than not, had about as much to do with public policy as whether your crowd or my crowd captured the most seats in high school student council.

This changed at the end of the nineteenth century, and it is here that the "informed citizen" dear to the Progressives makes his appearance. Reformers sought to make elections "educational" and to insulate the independent, rational citizen from the distorting enthusiasms of party. In the 1880s, political campaigns began to shift from parades to pamphlets, and so put a premium on literacy; in the early 1900s, non-partisan municipal elections, presidential primaries, and the initiative and referendum imposed more challenging cognitive tasks on prospective voters than ever before. Let me just take as emblematic the reform known as the "Australian ballot." This was the state-printed rather than party-printed ballot Americans still use today. It swept the country beginning in 1888; by 1892, most states employed it. The Australian ballot shifted the center of political gravity from party to voter. The new ballot asked voters *to make a choice among alternatives* rather than to perform an act of affiliation with a group. It elevated the individual, educated, rational voter as the model citizen. It helped political participation become more cognitive and less visceral, more intellectually demanding and a lot less fun. The large voting public of the late nineteenth century, with voter turn-out in the north routinely at 70 to 80 percent, became the vanishing public of the 1920s, with turn-out under 50 percent.[30]

Not incidentally, journalism changed at the same time. More and more newspapers claimed independence from political parties. More and more reporters began to pride themselves on factuality rather than partisan loyalty. More and more of them sought careers independent of political ambition. More and more political coverage reported political events in Washington not chronologically but with a "summary lead" and an "inverted pyramid" form in which the reporters, on their own non-partisan authority, determined what was most important in the event covered.

There were several problematic features of the new model of the informed citizen. First, it was from its beginnings racist and anti-immigrant. This aspect of informed citizenship can be rejected without surrendering the basic concept that citizens should learn candidates' positions and vote on the basis of information about the major issues before the nation. What is more inextricably part of the American notion of an informed electorate is a second problematic feature – that it is an explicit rejection of partisan politics and the intertwining of parties with every facet of daily life in cities. Reformers sought to cripple political parties. They branded them corrupters of democratic life, not contributors to it. They challenged the machines. This anti-party feature of the Progressive Era citizenship ideal has suffused our political thought and shaped our political imagination ever since. A century before Jeffords and McCain, the ideological foundations that would lead to their praise were laid.

The Progressive idea of the informed citizen is at war not only with the model of partisan citizenship that preceded it, but also with the most important model of citizenship that emerged later, a model of the irreverent, rights-conscious citizen, one who not only votes but litigates, not only litigates, but demonstrates and participates in social movements. This fourth stage of American citizenship added the courthouse and the street to the polling place as arenas of civic participation. Political movements and political organizations that, in the past, had only legislative points of access to political power found, in the power of political spectacle and in the judicial system, alternative routes to their goals.

Where do journalists affirm and endorse such acts of citizenship? There is journalistic sympathy for due process. Journalists challenge high-handedness. But despite love of "grass roots" activity, journalists are ambivalent about demonstrations, invariably wondering if and when they will descend to violence. Nor is there much sympathy for citizens who seek redress of grievances through litigation. On the contrary, as recent research demonstrates, the news media systematically and willingly side with corporations against individuals who sue them for personal injury. This is not because journalists love corporations or hate individuals but because they are drawn to outrageous stories that a conservative tort reform lobby drops into their laps.[31]

The rhetoric of rights, of course, is all around us now. But a wide variety of scholars and scolds, both left and right, now tell us to get past all this "rights talk" and get back to the more sturdy citizenship of responsibilities – voting, serving, informing ourselves, sacrificing. But the retreat from rights talk is hasty and ill considered. What really needs reconsideration is our century-old Progressive Era model of the informed citizen. It should be reformulated – to be less exclusivist, recognizing a variety of forms of political knowledge, not just those a political scientist or pollster would approve. It should be less antagonistic toward parties. It should be more attuned to the variety of ways people do politics, including making use of the courtroom as well as the voting booth. It should entertain the striking formulation of legal scholar Richard Abel – "To assert a legal claim is to perform a vital civic obligation."[32]

Instead, American journalism – and to a large degree American political thought generally – rests still in Progressive ideas. The implicit political model American journalists typically hold presumes the rational-choice, civic-duty, anti-party version of the voter at the polling place. There is little in self-conscious journalistic thought that acknowledges, as the founding fathers did, the values of social trust. There is little in journalistic thinking today but contempt for political parties, yet no idea of what alternative associational forms could adequately organize political representation. And there is little attention paid to the implications of a rights-conscious citizenship, except a tendency to take the proliferation of rights-claims against the government as a sign of selfishness, "NIMBYism," and general moral decline.

The vision of American journalism is a noble one: to provide the information, without fear or favor, that citizens can use to make the decisions to govern society, especially decisions about what candidates to vote for and what policies to support. However, this is not the only model of journalism and of citizenship consistent with democracy, and not even the only one to have supported democracy in the United States. Indeed, it is not the only model journalists practice today, but it is the only one journalists routinely recognize.

In practice, journalists are committed to much more than neutral transmission of relevant political facts. They are also committed to making news interesting – that is, to entertaining and engaging citizens as well as informing them, drawing them into politics rather than assuming that they come to the newspaper or television or webpage with interests and motivations fully formed. Journalists are also committed – to different degrees – to a watchdog function, investigating public officials to be sure that they are not betraying the public trust. As I argue in Chapter 2, the function of "transmitting relevant political information" is not inconsistent with the function of investigation, but it is not the same. In the watchdog model of journalism, the political world needs to be probed, not just described; it is not just a complicated world difficult to analyze but a devious world, intent on resisting discovery.

The aims of journalism do not stop here, either. Some journalists today – like almost all journalists in the nineteenth century in the United States – are avowedly partisan. As such, they promote a consistent and coherent view of the world from the perspective of a single political standpoint. Advocacy journalism of this sort is not only an effort to inform but an exhortation or incitement to participate. Other journalists aspire to what is sometimes called "explanatory journalism," where social science, rather than political advocacy, is the model. Not only do media organizations commission and analyze political polls, perhaps the most obvious domain where journalists practice social science, but they sometimes engage in very elaborate studies that, in another domain, might earn them an advanced degree in economics or sociology. The *New York Times*, in the first half of 2006, for instance, ran a major series on the social distribution of diabetes in New York, another on the lives of Muslims in New York, a story that measured the impact of parental notification laws on teenager abortion rates in states with such laws, and another story examining with a social scientific research design how people who fled their homes in Mississippi and Louisiana after Hurricane Katrina and settled elsewhere were faring economically and socially six months later.[33] All of these stories are political or politically relevant stories that represent an ambition that goes well beyond "covering" political events.

All of this is to suggest that journalists practice a more complex and more interesting journalism than they preach; likewise, they have developed a sense of politics more encompassing and less rigidly Progressive than they demonstrate in stories from the campaign trail or from Washington, DC. It could be an exercise of great value for journalists to think through their own political presuppositions and to rethink whether they have become conceptual fetters that should be removed.

7

What's unusual about covering politics as usual

The September 28, 2001 *New York Times* marked the end of the moment of overwhelming consensus in post-September 11 journalism. Of course, even months later, some of the patriotic fervor and the sense of national unity that burst forth after September 11 survived in journalism as in American society generally, but only as one element of national politics and political reporting, not as the whole thing.

On September 28 the *Times* ran a front-page story, "In Patriotic Time, Dissent is Muted," that recounted the fate that had befallen Americans, both prominent and obscure, who had not toed the patriotic line.[1] At least two small-town journalists had been fired for impolitic expression, and several corporations withdrew their sponsorship of Bill Maher's ABC television political satire show *Politically Incorrect*. In another front-page story, Washington correspondent Robin Toner wrote of the decline of bipartisanship after its initial rush and of how the Congress "is taking a second look – and a third and a fourth – at the administration's proposals for new law enforcement powers to fight terrorism."[2]

This was not the end of news of dissent and contention in the wake of the terrorist attack. A story from San Francisco reported how Japanese-Americans, remembering the internment camps of World War II, took it upon themselves to speak out against attacks on Arab-Americans.[3] A local story reported that some Americans responded to September 11 with newly devised charity scams to exploit the generous spirit of their fellow citizens.[4] Another local story reported that 8,000 frustrated residents were still displaced from their apartments near the World Trade Center. For some of them, "the mood has turned to anger." The residents were reported to be highly critical of the city administration.[5]

Then there was Mayor Rudolph Giuliani. In the first days of the crisis, Giuliani arose as a city and national hero. He acted with dignity, calm, tireless energy, and deep humanity. A news analysis on September 14 said as much, observing that Giuliani had taken charge of the city's response from the very first moments:

> Acting at once as chief operating officer of the city – personally monitoring, for instance, how many pounds of debris have been removed by the hour to securing low-interest loans to rebuild the city – to city psychologist, trying to assure a grief-stricken and terrified population that they are safe and that he knows they are hurting, the mayor has almost unilaterally managed to create the sense that the city and by its proxy, the nation, are scratching their way back to normalcy.

The ungainly length of that sentence accurately represents the breathless awe in which people who once criticized the mayor now regarded him.[6]

On September 28, however, the newspaper was no longer in awe. The *Times'* man-about-town columnist, John Tierney, laid into Giuliani's plan to stay on as mayor for three months past the end of his term of office. Giuliani had proposed this to the three leading candidates seeking to replace him and, appallingly, two of them accepted it without worrying over the fact that they had no legal authority to do so. "You might think," Tierney wrote, "that it's delusional of him now to believe that the city can't get along without him next year. But don't underestimate his sincerity. Mr. Giuliani is quite capable of believing himself indispensable."[7] Nor was this all. In a sharply worded lead editorial, the *Times* declared its views on the Mayor's extra-legal plan to remain in office: "This is a terrible idea."[8]

The American news media did an extraordinary job in the wake of September 11. The work of the *New York Times* staff was little short of miraculous in covering the terrorist attacks and their aftermath intensely, humanly, and in large measure fairly. I myself did not recognize this immediately. Although I normally read the *Times* along with my local newspaper daily, in the first few days after September 11, like most of my fellow citizens, I watched television obsessively. It took me a week to realize the *Times* was up to something extraordinary. On Tuesday, September 18, the regular "Science Times" Tuesday section ran stories on every conceivable scientific facet of the tragedy – the engineering task of clearing debris without risking the foundations of neighboring buildings;[9] the engineering task of building skyscrapers in the future less vulnerable to airplanes;[10] the adaptive advantage of altruism in evolutionary perspective;[11] the question of whether barring asbestos from buildings had reduced the Trade Centers' capacity to withstand the fires that destroyed them;[12] the dangers of dust inhalation in lower Manhattan;[13] how to make jet fuel safer;[14] two first-hand accounts by physicians who both happened to be regular contributors to the *Times'* Science section and providers of emergency medicine at Bellevue Hospital and at Ground Zero on September 11;[15] the problems for blood banks of maintaining a blood supply;[16] the ways individuals cope with trauma[17] – all in separate, detailed stories that no one could have imagined when the section was originally planned.

This terrible tragedy for the world proved a great opportunity for journalism. People were willing to watch and read far beyond what they normally absorb. Journalism is a curriculum, as James Carey has suggested, with breaking news only the intro. course.[18] After that comes the human interest side-bar, the biographical sketch of a person in the news, news analysis, the lengthy magazine piece, later the book. After September 11, many people were prepared to go well beyond the intro. course. At the same time, journalists expanded the curriculum with the invention of new forms of reportage, notably the *New York Times'* poignant quasi-obituaries for the people killed in New York. Through December 31, 2001, these obituaries were printed as part of the *Times'* special news section devoted exclusively to news related to September 11 and terrorism, "A Nation Challenged."

It is surprising, in retrospect, how quickly this remarkable series of obituaries emerged. On Saturday, September 15, their first installment ran under the heading, "Among the Missing." The next day the heading was "After the Attack: Portraits of Grief," and "Portraits of Grief" would be the permanent head, still in use six months later. Without directly referring to what was clearly becoming a series, the *Times* editorialized on Sunday, September 16: "The Faces Emerge." The editorial called attention to the fliers posted across New York seeking information on missing friends and relatives. It called attention to the obituaries beginning to appear in newspapers across the country. It observed the arbitrariness of who was caught in the World Trade Center that day and who was not, and it called for readers to pay attention to:

> a remarkably precious opportunity to witness a portrait of this nation assembled out of memories and pictures, out of the efforts of everyday people to explain in everyday words who it is they lost on Tuesday. They hold out their photographs to strangers and television cameras. The faces looking out of those pictures could not have imagined knowing what we know now. You can tell it by the way they smile.[19]

Each day "A Nation Challenged" featured an interpretive news summary at the bottom of the first page. This was another innovation, a fairly free-form structure, sometimes more essay than news, as on December 26 when Jane Gross wrote: "Holidays have come and gone, none more poignant than this first Christmas in a changed world, a changed city, where no amount of tinsel can replace the sparkle of nearly 3,000 lost lives. But hesitantly, reluctantly, inevitably people are inching toward more normal lives, groping for wisdom and perspective."[20] Gross fell into an elegiac tone, worlds away from ordinary *Times* prose. The tone of the "Portraits of Grief" was even more unusual. These portraits were not the formal, heavy obituaries readers are used to but quick-sketches, efforts not to list family and survivors but to suggest a spark of life that made each person special or different. Their stylistic heritage is more from the feature story than from obituary writing, but they represent a new hybrid, a kind of haiku obit. They are a form of journalism as tribute, journalism as homage, journalism as witness, journalism as solace, and journalism aspiring to art.

The "A Nation Challenged" section was discontinued at the end of the calendar year. The ushering in of 2002 seemed a fitting occasion to return to normal, with all the mixed feelings that "returning to normal" brings to a family, or nation, in mourning.

Despite the exceptional quality of the journalism that developed so quickly after September 11, I found that the *New York Times* edition of September 28 came as a great relief. For two very long weeks, journalists wrote in a way that emphasized not only factual accuracy and analytical power but human connection to their community. And still, a return to reporting a kind of politics in a style that was reporting as usual felt redemptive, as if a fever had just broken after a prolonged illness. Why? Where is the comfort in the normality of political reporting?

Syndicated columnist Ellen Goodman wrote on December 7, "When terrorists struck on Sept. 11, there was only one side. No editor demanded a quote from someone saying why it was fine to fly airplanes into buildings. No one expected reporters to take an 'objective' view of the terrorists."[21] While criticizing the Fox News Channel for slanted, jingoistic coverage, Goodman found herself nonetheless ready to embrace the mantra of Fox News Director Roger Ailes: "be accurate, be fair, be American."

The same day, broadcast anchorman Tom Brokaw wrote a newspaper column comparing September 11, 2001, and December 7, 1941, the date of the Japanese attack on Pearl Harbor. Among the similarities he noted was the centrality of the news media: "On that long ago Sunday and the more recent Tuesday, Americans were glued to news broadcasts, bringing this vast land to a standstill." In both cases, he observes, "the nation bonded electronically."[22]

September 11 blew the fuses of preconceived ideas about journalism and just about everything else. Journalists ran on instinct, on professionalism and did their best to get the story, to get to the scene, to cover the facts, to interview the president, the mayor, the police chief, the emergency room physician, the wounded, the witness. They reported too many rumors but they made their corrections. They did not have a language for the terrorism at first. Tragedy. Atrocity. Yes. But is this war? Or is this criminal activity? Where is responsibility? Where is resolution? The president spoke angrily, perhaps even recklessly, but backed off. Republicans called for increased federal power in the economy, not hands off. Democrats supported greater police and military authority. The public, somewhat skeptical of President George W. Bush, rallied behind him. And then what? And what happened to journalism?

Two things happened immediately and with some enduring effect. First, journalism moved quickly away from its standard handling of political events as part of what Daniel Hallin has termed the "sphere of legitimate controversy."[23] Hallin's conceptualization is useful and clarifying. He argues in his influential study of the media in Vietnam that journalism's commitment to objectivity has always been compartmentalized. That is, within a certain sphere – the sphere of legitimate controversy – journalists seek conscientiously to be balanced and objective. But there is also a "sphere of consensus" in which journalists feel free to invoke a generalized "we" and to take for granted shared values and shared assumptions.[24] When President Kennedy was assassinated, no journalist felt obliged to seek out sources to praise the assassin as well as to condemn him. In fact, there were Americans who initially exulted in the assassination, but journalists did not feel any obligation to represent them as legitimate voices in news coverage. The assassination was treated as a national tragedy and the media audience was addressed as part of a large national family that had suffered a grievous blow.

Hallin points also to a third sphere, a "sphere of deviance," where journalists also depart from standard norms of objective reporting and feel authorized to treat as marginal, laughable, dangerous, or ridiculous individuals and groups who fall far outside a range of variation taken as legitimate.[25] Pre-teen girls swooning over adolescent rock stars can be presented in a mocking or condescending tone (can they be presented in any other way?) that would never be appropriate for covering members of Congress. A vegetarian or temperance candidate for president can be presented as a light side-note to the seriousness of the main arena of politics.

After September 11, journalists felt thrust into the sphere of consensus. Neither deferential objectivity nor tough, assertive professionalism, modes appropriate to covering legitimate controversies, seemed adequate to the moment. Journalism as an instrument of providing information and analysis of public affairs did not seem enough. And so journalists shifted modes as if changing to another musical key or switching to a different language. They moved toward the sphere of consensus. They moved into what might even be called a priestly or pastoral mode. The tone of detached neutrality was replaced by a quiet, solemn tone, as if speaking at a funeral. There is no doubt much ill that could be spoken of the dead. Certainly there is much ill that could be spoken of the president and the previous president and the Congress, all of whom largely ignored the reports on terrorism, conscientiously written and edited and published and then put on the back burner – as did most of the media, for that matter.[26] All of this unfolded while President Bush focused his energies on a crusade for $300 tax rebates. Criticism of the short-sightedness of national leadership was, at most, muted. Journalists were not out to find scapegoats. It was just not appropriate at a time of national mourning.

Instead, post-September 11 journalism sought to provide comfort or reassurance, not just information or analysis. One journalist at the *Times* explained that the point of the "Portraits of Grief" was to give solace to the families of the victims. But, as journalist and media critic James Fallows observed, "the real significance of this series is clearly to give solace to a community – not simply the community of New York or those who knew the victims personally but the entire national community for which the remembrances have become a powerful sacrament." Fallows not only praised the *Times* for the "Portraits of Grief" but mischievously observed that this was exactly the sort of "public journalism" that *Times* editor Howell Raines had vigorously condemned. That is, it was a journalism that "stopped kidding itself about its ability to remain detached from and objective about public life. It is trying to help its city and its nation and it is succeeding."[27]

There are three occasions when US journalists instinctively and willingly abandon the effort to report from a neutral stance. In moments of tragedy, journalists assume a pastoral role. On television, correspondents adopt quiet, even reverent tones, an air of solemnity. This is evident, for instance, in news coverage of assassinations of political leaders, in state funerals, and since September 11 in coverage of the mourning of the victims.

Second, in moments of public danger, journalists replace professional objectivity with neighborly reassurance, whether danger comes from terrorists or hurricanes. They seek to offer practical guidance and to communicate fellow feeling. They become part of a public health campaign, not just a public information system.

Third, journalists also reject neutrality during threats to national security. When they are convinced that national security is at risk, they willingly withhold or temper their reports. American journalists did so at the time of the Bay of Pigs invasion of Cuba in 1961, for example, and on other occasions where releasing information might put American military forces in harm's way.

September 11 combined all three moments into one: tragedy, public danger, and a grave threat to national security. Journalists did not have to be instructed to speak reverently of the victims of the terrorist attacks. They did not have to be directed to pronounce the fire fighters and police officers at the World Trade Center heroes. They did not have to be commanded to reassure citizens when anthrax infection threatened public panic. In tragedy, public danger, and threats to national security, there are no "sides." We are all in it together. Much reporting after September 11 turned toward a prose of solidarity rather than a prose of information.

The second thing that happened to journalism happened to the journalists themselves and came perhaps as something of a revelation to them: they liked the new intimacy of the consensual "we." They felt connected and important to their audience. They felt appreciated as they rarely do. Many American journalists who reported about September 11 and later the war in Afghanistan felt good about their work. "At last!" they seemed to sigh; "This is what journalism is about! This is why I am a journalist!" Nick Spangler, on September 11 a journalism student at Columbia on an election-day assignment (September 11 was to be the mayoral primary in New York) for a reporting class, found himself near Ground Zero when the terrorists attacked. He took his camera and notepad and covered what he could. "I felt an intense passion in those hours, an exaltation," he later wrote: "I felt alone at the center of the world. All details became iconic and crucial. I tried to record everything."[28] *New York Times* reporter Katherine Finkelstein got to Ground Zero before the towers collapsed and stayed there for forty hours. A police officer gave her his pen when she lost hers; she wrote down a list of what supplies the medics needed to help them. She was reporting, but not as an outsider. She was performing a community service, as many (but not all) around her recognized in befriending her; she represented an institution and a function that could help.[29] Even the most professional, detached reporting could feel like a service to the country's highest ideals, as when reporters wrote stories on critics of American policy who had suffered angry rebuke or on Muslim Americans who were assaulted by stupid and vengeful fellow citizens.

Not incidentally, even print journalists found occasion to praise their broadcast colleagues. There was a "new, if fleeting, dignity" that September 11 conferred on broadcast journalism, wrote Orville Schell, Dean of the School of Journalism at the University of California, Berkeley. He observed that the broadcast media "helped inform and calm us so that we

could keep some part of our critical faculties in abeyance to think reasonably about what had befallen us. The result has been an unprecedented
sense of togetherness and common purpose for which we owe a profound
debt of thanks to television and radio."[30] "For one week there was no race,
just the human race," said *New York Times* reporter Charlie LeDuff. He
was obviously moved by covering the recovery efforts at Ground Zero as
construction workers, medical personnel, migrant workers, hundreds of
volunteers went to work. "You were surrounded by humanity down there,"
he told his journalism school alumni newsletter, "It was inspiring to
watch."[31]

Yes, it was, even at a distance. And everyone seemed to be watching
and, in whatever way they could, participating. I got a form letter from my
brokerage: "Dear Valued Client: On Tuesday September 11, many of us
who worked at The World Trade Center returned home to our loved ones.
Sadly, all of us did not." I even received a holiday season form letter from
my dentist: "Dear Friends, Many people have been affected by the terrible
events of the recent past." It promoted a teeth whitening procedure, profits
from which would be donated to the Red Cross. People in my office made
sure that I, as a college administrator, wore an American flag on my lapel.
I appreciated the gesture and I felt solidarity with the office staff as I wore
it. I attended memorial services at the university and I sang "God Bless
America" with the others. The media were, for a week or two, only the tip
of the communicative iceberg. Everyone called friends and family in New
York. Everyone spoke about the attacks to their children, or worked out
for themselves why they would not speak to them; everyone shared the
TV with the kids or shielded them from it self-consciously. My next-door
neighbor is a firefighter, and I looked at him with new regard.

But now, my dentist is again my dentist, not my comrade, and my
neighbor is again my neighbor. Normality is in the United States the
enemy of patriotism, not its underpinning. Pastoral journalism cannot be
sustained. It seeks to offer reassurance, not information; it seeks to speak
to and for a unified people rather than a people divided by conflict and
interested in conflict; it seeks to build community rather than to inform it.
This is not peculiar to the United States. Up to the day he was assassinated,
Israel's Prime Minister Yitzhak Rabin was a politician. The next day he
was a statesman, a martyr, and a saint. For a time after his death, it was
not possible to criticize him in the press.[32] Not because there was censorship from outside but because journalists knew, internally and intuitively,
that criticism would be unseemly.

Journalism after September 11 showed that it could not only inform but
console, not only make us think but make us cry. We learned deeper truths
than journalism is ordinarily prepared to handle, and one of these truths is

about journalism itself – that it never stands entirely outside the community it reports on.

But the moment passed. It passed before the media were prepared to let go of it. The result is that the neon banners on television like "America Under Siege" or "America Strikes Back" or the other slogans used by print and broadcast but most gratingly by television outlasted their usefulness. They fairly quickly felt like marketing, not journalism. They seemed forced, false, cloying, self-aggrandizing, jingoistic. Likewise, the labeling of anti-terrorist measures as the "USA Patriot Act" (a sophomorically clever acronym for legislation labeled "Uniting and Strengthening America by Providing Appropriate Tools Required to Intercept and Obstruct Terrorism") seemed embarrassing. This was not so at first, not in the heat of the shattering moment, but it became so soon enough.

Somewhere in late September, even as preparations for the war in Afghanistan mounted, the unquestioning "we" began to dissolve. "I hate the first-person plural . . . I grew up with 'we' and 'us': in the kindergarten, at school, in the pioneer and youth organisations, in the community, at work," writes Slavenka Drakulic of life in Yugoslavia: "I grew up listening to the speeches of politicians saying, 'Comrades, we must . . .' and with these comrades, we did what we were told, because we did not exist in any other grammatical form."[33]

The "we" and the "us" turned up repeatedly in news accounts of September 11. That there was cause for this, one cannot doubt. The terrorist attack was a clear message that, from the perspective of a disciplined, planful, cruelly single-minded suicidal hijacker, the only good American was a dead one. The friends and admirers of these terrorists would shed no tears over those who died, rich and poor, American and foreigner, Christian, Jew, and Muslim. The victims included Americans of old stock and newly arrived immigrants. No terrorist could see inscribed in the name of one of the most severely decimated brokerage houses, Cantor and Fitzgerald, an extraordinary symbol of some of the best of the past century of American history, the marriage of two ethnic groups, of two religious groups, Jew and Catholic, both of them widely treated as dirt just a hundred years ago. The twin towers were not only about world trade, that was only their business; they were about the bargaining and contracts one human being makes with another, the hopes and loves of individuals reaching out to one another from their parochial backgrounds through commerce, desire, love, ambition, and comradeship.

So it is easy to recognize all that the adoption of a "we" affirmed in post-September 11 journalism. It is easy to accept that American flags appeared on the lapels of reporters and local TV anchors and flew over the headquarters of news organizations.

At the same time, how can one be an American journalist and a patriot simultaneously? In World War II, this question did not arise. In that war, the US government treated reporting as "essential service" and grounds for exemption from the military draft, just like work in defense plants. Journalists and government officials alike took reporting to be a weapon in the war. In the Korean war, reporters accompanying UN troops traded access to information for agreement not to criticize the troops. Only in Vietnam, and then rather late in the war, did "our war" become "the war."[34] Journalists took up a professional detachment rather than a patriotic deference to military authority. Ever since, US journalists have sought maximum access to information during war and have chafed at military information control and censorship.

Journalism under normal circumstances is something else again. Under normal circumstances, American society operates with security taken for granted, with public danger at bay, and with tragedy a matter of private circumstance rather than public sharing. Under normal circumstances, our lives are both enriched and complicated by dissent and conflict. Under normal circumstances, dissent and conflict enhance and express the nation's democratic aspirations rather than undermine their possibility. Under normal circumstances, citizens are both drawn to and put off by the self-serving-ness and the arrogance and the guile of political language. Under normal circumstances, journalists serve society by adhering to their professional ideals and not by worrying too much over how they might assuage the hurts of their communities.

Covering politics as usual means operating in an atmosphere of conflict and division. It means learning to live with a relatively high level of noise, of raised voices, of fists shaking in anger, of a rhetoric of outrage and of outrageous rhetoric. It means learning to manage the histrionics of competition, rivalry, and even a degree of skulduggery. This is not everybody's cup of tea. Politics *is* dirty. That is something to work with, however, not to fear. It drives people to find community and solidarity in other spheres, not in a national politics.

There is much to cherish in this. Politics should serve society, not command it. It should enlarge and enrich and secure the space for human life to prosper in common. Part of what was striking about the patriotic outburst after September 11 is that it was so chastened. People spoke words they will (or should) regret, the Reverend Jerry Falwell's taking first prize. But there were not many, and remarkably few from the nation's elected leaders. There was reserve and resolve and a self-conscious awareness that patriotic fervor was appropriate and necessary but also dangerous. This was certainly true in the media where, within days, prominently placed news reports raised concerns about how national security could be enhanced without unduly damaging the civil liberties that are part of America's very definition of itself.[35]

So, as much as I admire the coverage the *New York Times* provided in the days after September 11, there was something profoundly reassuring in that edition of September 28. It was reassuring that Democrats and Republicans were arguing with each other in Congress, that journalists were on Mayor Giuliani's back, that there was resistance when he tried to transform his demi-god status into a demagogue's, that downtown Manhattan residents were bitching at the city bureaucracy, that Japanese-Americans out of their own deep injury at the hands of the American government were looking out for Arab-Americans, that punitive responses to those who dissented from the consensus of the moment were being criticized.

It was wonderful to see all that messiness again, all that conflict, all that stuff that makes people turn in disgust from the back-biting, back-stabbing, power-grabbing low-down of politics. Media scholars have been apt in recent years to complain that standard political reporting in the American press is cynical, indicating between the lines that politicians are motivated invariably by the desire for office or re-election, not by actual conviction about anything beyond their own careers.[36] I am among those who have complained.[37] Well, the cynicism is surely there, but it represents more democratic virtue and vigor than critics have allowed.

8

The anarchy of events and the anxiety of story telling

At meetings I have attended that bring together journalists and social scientists, the scholars insist that news is a social construction, that journalists and the organizations they work for make news. The journalists, horrified by what they take to be a slander, insist that, no, they just report what they see. For a long time I thought the journalists were naïve. Now I have come to think it is the scholars who are naïve.

Of course, news *is* socially constructed. In this the scholars are correct. Journalists make news. But they do not make it up. News is socially constructed, but it is constructed out of Something, not out of whole cloth. And the Somethings that journalists are most sensitive to and responsive to and that scholarship has barely begun to think about are what we call "events." Journalists respond to events that they often have not anticipated and do not understand. Their task is to fit those events into comprehensible categories and to narrate them in comprehensible ways, to tame them, to socially reconstruct them, if you will.

But they fail. Events are too cunning for journalists or for any of us. That is why they remain interesting, remarkable, newsworthy. Journalists make their own stories but not from materials they have personally selected. Materials are thrust upon them. A preoccupation with unpredictable events keeps something uncontrollable at the forefront of journalism. The archetypal news story, the kind that makes a career, the sort every reporter longs for, is unroutinized and unrehearsed. This gives journalism its recurrent anarchic potential. And it is built into the very bloodstream of news organizations, it is the circulatory system that keeps the enterprise oxygenated.

All of us want to tame the anarchy of events. The entire insurance industry rests on this desire. So does the legal institution of contract, the long-term fixed-interest home mortgage, the rules of protocol in diplomacy, the practice of etiquette in formal and informal social behavior, the elaborate coaching and training it takes to produce a concert violinist, an actor on a stage, or a professional athlete. Presidents and prime ministers practice answering questions before news conferences. We live by these institutions and conventions, endure this schooling and coaching, steel ourselves for performance, all to make our lives more predictable and more controlled.

People outsource some of this event-taming activity to journalists. How do journalists tame the raw material that confronts them on a daily basis, the anarchy of events in the world, the daily renewal of accidents, events, dramas, and incidents that yesterday could not have been predicted? True, we all knew yesterday that today would bring homicides, house breakings, and natural disasters, but we could not predict who, or where, or any of the details. Sports reporters know ahead of time that a horse race will produce one story of triumph and eight or nine of disappointment and defeat, but they cannot say which horse will be the subject of which narrative.

So how do journalists handle the anarchy of events? There are two kinds of answers to this question. The first answer is that journalists organize their work lives to manage events. They do this in a variety of well-recognized ways, most notably by establishing on-going relations with politicians and public bureaucracies, from the police department to the coroner's office to the public information officers and press secretaries at City Hall, the leading hospitals and universities, and so on. News-gathering on a daily basis means maintaining contact with the organizations that most reliably produce useable items of news, and cultivating relations with those sources that are closest to and most knowledgeable about the regular news-makers. The telephone, even in the age of the Internet, is the indispensable tool.[1]

The second answer is that journalists handle the anarchy of events by depending on available cultural resources, the treasurehouse of tropes, narrative forms, resonant mythic forms and frames of their culture. They assimilate the new, apparently novel, unique, unprecedented event to the familiar old ways of understanding the world. A car is a horseless carriage. The Internet is a digital town hall meeting or an information superhighway or an electronic frontier.

Efforts to fit the news to an old literary or journalistic trope, critics routinely argue, are inappropriate. They simplify. They force us to communicate through stereotypes. They prematurely fit the actors on the scene into white hats and black hats. This is the argument, for instance, advanced in Elisabeth Anker's *Journal of Communication* paper on the melodramatic reporting of September 11 on Fox News. Anker offers a lucid account of what melodrama is and then shows by a close analysis of one hour of Fox News that Fox presented Al Qaeda's attacks on New York and Washington melodramatically, fostering a Manichean view of the world in which Islamic terrorists represent evil and the World Trade Towers represent America's innocence and victimhood. Anker objects to this. For her, it oversimplifies. It prevents thoughtfulness. For Anker, "we must begin to question the seductions of this national self-understanding that feeds on an attachment to victimization and generates vengeful heroism."[2]

Anker chooses not to criticize the seductions of radical Islam's self-understanding that fed on an attachment to victimization and generated vengeful heroism. She treats Al Qaeda's attack as an entirely neutral or ambiguous event that Fox News prematurely turned to melodrama, reflecting and reinforcing a dangerous American self-understanding. But the attack on 9/11 was not an earthquake or tsunami. It was a human act, painstakingly planned over a period of years. It was generated by a profoundly Manichean world-view. Osama bin Laden takes the gold medal as the contemporary world's most successful purveyor and performer of melodrama. The event suggested melodrama more than the availability of melodrama among our cultural categories froze the event into the form in which it is routinely narrated.

Anker implies that melodrama is how the American media see – and inappropriately see – the world. But journalists tell non-Manichean stories all the time. Is Ariel Sharon good or bad? Hero or villain? Vladimir Putin? Tony Blair? Jacques Chirac? Hosni Mubarak? The US news media do not present any of them in melodramatic terms. Sports reporting has heroes but rarely enemies. Human interest stories often draw our attention to ironies and oddities and phenomena that betray our expectations, but they, too, rarely offer up enemies.

Reporting immediately after 9/11 *did* tend to what I have called (in Chapter 7) a journalism of solidarity, rather than a journalism of detachment. It did tend to divide the world into "us" and "them." Fox was not alone in its melodramatic imagination. In leading news organizations, however, this was not a permanent or even a long-term condition. The *New York Times* (as indicated in detail in Chapter 7), returned to reporting as usual within weeks. On September 28, the *Times* reported that Democrats and Republicans in Congress were arguing about how to fight terrorism; an editorial condemned Mayor Rudolph Giuliani for his proposal to remain as mayor for three months past the end of his term; a news story found that New Yorkers displaced from homes and offices near the site of the World Trade Towers were moaning to city bureaucrats about their fate and delays in restoring them to a normal life; a front-page report assembled scattered but scary cases where overzealous patriotism caused harm to dissenters; and still another story reported that charity scams were multiplying to exploit the post-9/11 generosity of many Americans. All of this in a single day's paper! It is not possible to read this one issue of the nation's most influential newspaper and still believe that the American media are drenched in a nationalistic, self-justifying melodramatic imagination.

Why did Fox News select melodrama as its cultural resource on the evening of September 11, 2001? Other news stories draw on other cultural resources. What other cultural categories or frames lie on the shelf, ready for use? Irony is one familiar narrative device in the news. Media scholar James Ettema recounts the ironic framework used throughout the mainstream American media in covering the 1992 killing of Yoshihiro Hattori.[3] Hattori was a 16-year-old Japanese exchange student in Louisiana who, on Halloween, wearing a Halloween costume, walked up to the wrong house, and unintentionally scared the woman who answered the door. She screamed for her husband, he charged out with a .44 Magnum and shouted "Freeze!" Hattori, not understanding that this meant he should stand still and submit to further instructions, walked forward and the man shot him fatally.

As Ettema shows, this senseless killing was presented as irony. As it was told and retold, it became the set-piece for a critique of American gun culture with the horrified Japanese responses from across the Pacific regularly and favorably included as part of the on-going tale. Irony became the platform for American moral self-criticism. With 9/11, as the story was told and retold, occasional self-critical doubts arose – "Why do they hate us so much?" stories – but generally the melodrama remained overpowering.

Neither melodrama nor irony stands in for all American news. Why was 9/11 framed as melodrama and Hattori's murder as irony? Could it have been reversed? Could the media have played up the irony that devastation was wreaked upon the United States under the guidance of a man that the United States supported when he worked to defeat the Soviets in Afghanistan? Could Hattori's story have been a melodrama of America protecting itself from invading hordes of Asian students? Or could it more plausibly have been a melodrama of a sick American culture of violence victimizing innocent youths? There were, in fact, elements of the latter in the news coverage, but the remorse of Hattori's killer made it difficult. The killing may ultimately have been related to a gun culture but immediately it was related to a misunderstanding, and misunderstandings are always ironic. It is not easy to picture the Hattori story as melodrama or 9/11 as irony. Journalists did not have an unhindered choice to root among their cultural resources and select whichever one suited them. I think they "naturally," without much thought, responded with the narrative frame that they believed fit the circumstances of the event before them.

The anxiety of journalistic story telling is double. It is an anxiety not only to identify what the story is but to do so in a way that does not lose the audience. This is not a matter of ratings or market research. It is a matter of tacit knowledge and tacit learning, shared human sympathies as they exist in a given society at a given time. Consider the remarks of Associated Press veteran Walter Mears, commenting on media criticism of 2004 campaign coverage. He writes, "There are too many excursions into trivia, too much play for the public opinion polls, too many words about who's ahead and who's behind. There's a reason. That is what people want to know. I have never been asked at a cocktail party to describe the positions of the candidates on the balance of payments problem. I am always asked which candidate is going to win the election at hand." For Mears, the horse race story does not get in the way of policy discussion but is the one feature of elections that makes policy discussion possible and appealing. "It seemed to me," he writes, "that the competition between candidates every fourth year – the horse race, if you want to use that terminology – provided an opportunity to report on the competition between their ideas. Write about issues in the abstract and you have position papers that will go widely unread. Write about the race between rival candidates and rival issues, and you have copy that will draw readers."[4] Elections are always attempts to simplify. They take persistent policy discussions, with no clear beginning and no clear end and many shades of gray and many variables and they bring it all down to a simple binary choice in two-party systems. (Multi-party elections also simplify, but not so completely.) It is not, in the end, a choice about policy but about leaders with a relationship to a set of issues. Democracy itself – at least democracy with a two-party system – not just news accounts of it, urges upon us stories of fateful rivalry.

I have written as if events are one thing – out there in the world – and telling about them in the media is a separate order of reality. This cuts against the grain of contemporary scholarship. And it is ultimately wrong because human perceptions and framings of the world do shape the world that then appears, by optical illusion, to act independently upon us. Still, for most practical purposes, it is reasonable to believe that there are events in the world we can shape, distort, reinterpret, but not fundamentally change. President Kennedy was killed by an assassin. There are lots of ways to read this fact but none of them restore John F. Kennedy to life. He really died.

Almost all media criticism and much media scholarship is fueled in part by an indignation about the gap between reality as the author conceives it and the representation or reduction of reality in the media. Anker objects to the moral import of a news frame that is inconsistent with her moral and political preferences. Ettema judges as benign or perhaps even beneficial the moralization of a story consistent with his own moral preferences. He understands, as Anker does not, that news is a multi-genre cultural form that draws on various conflicting and disparate cultural resources, and that these resources enable journalists sometimes to shed a critical light on American institutions. Smug and self-aggrandizing coverage is not foreordained.

American journalists write melodramatically here, ironically there, comically somewhere else, reverently or piously in some other contexts. They make choices from a variety of narrative forms and conventions. The next task is to understand how they make these choices, to understand why melodrama seems to be almost inevitable here and irony almost irresistible there. I do not have the answer to this question. I only suggest that the answer will not be wholly independent of features that inhere in the reported events themselves.

9

Why conversation is not the soul of democracy

The notion of "civil society" and "the public sphere" have drawn attention to the character of "talk" as a constitutive feature of democracy. When Jürgen Habermas writes that "a portion of the public sphere comes into being in every conversation in which private individuals assemble to form a public body," conversation is granted an exceedingly important political role.[1] If democracy is, as it has often been called, government by discussion, or, more precisely, "government by rational and free public discussion among legally equal citizens," conversation must lie close to its heart.[2]

This was certainly the view of John Dewey. For him, talk was the central feature of democratic life. The chief requirement for revitalizing public life, he wrote in 1927, was "the improvement of the methods and conditions of debate, discussion and persuasion. That is *the* problem of the public."[3] Such high authority notwithstanding, it is this claim that I want to criticize. I do so in a friendly spirit – that is, I am criticizing a notion I myself find very appealing. But I also think it has been misleading, perhaps dangerously so.

The place of conversation in democracy

One does not have to search far today to find views that place conversation at the center of democratic life. David Simpson even speaks of a "cult of 'conversation'" today. There is a veritable obsession with the term. It can be found all over the academic landscape – in postmodernist philosophy, in communitarian social criticism, in the public journalism movement, and elsewhere. It is to be found in liberal critics of the mass media and in philosophers of discursive democracy. It is central to Richard Rorty's critique of scientific and philosophical certainty. What we can "know," for Rorty, is only what we can come to in on-going conversation with others, rather than in an encounter with a nature beyond human interaction. Rorty, Michael Oakeshott, and Hans-Georg Gadamer all turn to "conversation" as a model of knowing. We are seeing, Simpson has observed, "the appearance of the conversational ideal in postmodern culture."[4]

In communication studies, James Carey has been especially eloquent in placing conversation at the center of public life and the restoration of a public at the heart of the contemporary task of democratic society. The public, he writes, is "a group of strangers that gathers to discuss the news." It is "a society of conversationalists or disputants, dependent upon printing for the dissemination of their ideas." This was the grand ideal of the public – and it existed in reality, in Carey's view, much as it does in Habermas. This "conversational public," as Carey puts it, was "a public of discussion and disputation independent of both the press and the State" and it "has pretty much been eviscerated in our time." In the twentieth century, as journalism became more "objective" according to its professional lights, the relationship of press and public disintegrated: "The press no longer facilitated or animated a public conversation for public conversation had disappeared." The press was no longer the background to the central task of conversation; any remaining conversation "was orchestrated by the press in the name of a superior knowledge and superior instruments of inquiry into just what was going on." For Carey, independent journalism, made all the worse by television, helped destroy political parties while opinion polling helped obscure genuine public opinion. The public arena shrank, and citizens had little choice but to be "consumers of politics or escapists from it."[5]

But what is – or what was or what might be – this ideal conversation at the very soul of democratic life? Are we to imagine it as a form of social life, spontaneous and free? This would seem to be an important part of what makes conversation central. But it would be wrong to assume that the spontaneous is the authentic or true. An emphasis on the spontaneous draws attention away from the contrivances necessary for democracy – indeed, it draws attention away from the fact that democracy is a contrivance. I will argue that democratic talk is not essentially spontaneous but essentially rule-governed, essentially *civil*, and unlike the kinds of conversation often held in highest esteem for their freedom and their wit, it is essentially oriented to *problem-solving*.

Are we to suppose that conversation is egalitarian? This is not necessarily so. An individual must have "cultural capital" to participate effectively in conversation. One might even argue that the actual relationship of talk and equality is not one of affinity but of paradox. The more that talk is among true equals, the more it fails to make assumptions clear, fails to state premises, fails to be accessible to all, lapses even into silence. The presumption of equality in conversation draws attention away from the fundamental problem of membership in democracy, of insiders and outsiders, and so precludes attention to the rules that make democracy possible for a pluralistic rather than a homogeneous population. What distinguishes democratic conversation, I want to suggest, is not equality but publicness. Democratic talk is not necessarily egalitarian but it is essentially *public*, and if this means that democratic talk is talk among people with different values and different backgrounds, it is also profoundly uncomfortable.

Ideas about conversation in the Western tradition can be traced back at least to Cicero, who wrote that private conversation should be easy-going, free of passions, free of gossip about people not present, and that it should include everyone and allow everyone a turn. Following Cicero, early modern Italian, French, and British advice literature on conversation stressed that conversation should be cooperative and egalitarian. Interruption, as French manuals of the seventeenth century reiterated, was wrong; so too was monopolizing the conversation. At the same time, spontaneity was urged, even if, ironically, it had to be premeditated. One authority recommended "hesitation and even an occasional clumsiness in order to preserve the illusion of spontaneity."[6]

Still, the egalitarian advice was within a context. There was also advice on the ways to speak to one's superiors and inferiors, and it did not have to be said at all that some people were outside the conversation. Spontaneity was encouraged – yes, but also advice on how to produce it. Cooperation – yes, but the early manuals also recognized the competitiveness in conversation and the desire to shine. Historian Peter Burke concludes that "a truly general theory of conversation should discuss the tension and the balance between the competitive and cooperative principles, between equality and hierarchy, between inclusion and exclusion, and between spontaneity and study, rather than placing all the weight on the first item in each of these pairs."[7]

Recognizing a tension between principles in conversation is one way to arrive at a more coherent and realistic view of conversation. I propose, alternatively, that two rather different ideals of conversation are intertwined and confused. One ideal could be termed the aesthetic model of conversation, the other the problem-solving model. The distinguishing feature of the aesthetic ideal is its insistence that conversation be nonutilitarian. In a conversation, as political philosopher Michael Oakeshott wrote, the aim is not inquiry, there is no hankering after a conclusion.

Neither informing nor persuading are crucial. Reasoning "is not sovereign" and conversation "does not compose an argument." Conversation has no end outside itself. It is "an unrehearsed intellectual adventure" and, "as with gambling, its significance lies neither in winning nor in losing, but in wagering."[8]

What is perhaps the most resonant part of Oakeshott's discussion of conversation is his notion that what human beings of a given age inherit in human civilization is not science or technology or an accumulating body of knowledge but

> a conversation, begun in the primeval forests and extended and made more articulate in the course of centuries. It is a conversation which goes on both in public and within each of ourselves. . . . It is the ability to participate in this conversation, and not the ability to reason cogently, to make discoveries about the world, or to contrive a better world, which distinguishes the human being from the animal and the civilized man from the barbarian.[9]

In this model, then, conversation is oriented to the pleasure of interacting with others in conversation itself; it is therefore contemporaneously social. But, further, as part of an on-going conversation over time, taking its materials from a long-term human tradition, it is also historically social.

In contrast, the problem-solving understanding of conversation finds the justification of talk in its practical relationship to the articulation of common ends. Popular voting, majority rule, and other indices of democracy are vouched for, John Dewey wrote, by the fact that "they involve a consultation and discussion which uncover social needs and troubles."[10] For Dewey, democracy could not exist without participation, and conversation was the hallmark of the participatory: "The connections of the ear with vital and out-going thought and emotion are immensely closer and more varied than those of the eye. Vision is a spectator; hearing is a participator."[11]

For Carey, similarly, although one senses in his writing an attraction to the pure pleasure of talk, the emphasis is on conversation as the workplace in which democracy happens if it happens at all. Conversation, for Carey, is dispute around the news, a discussion of the issues of the day. It is the back-and-forth out of which a democratic public realizes itself. Carey is in some respects critical of Dewey, particularly his failure to think through questions of power present in talk, and Carey's distrust of experts in democracy does not come to terms with Dewey's faith in science as the fundamental knowledge-base for democratic life. But, on the whole, Carey's voice in communication studies has been one championing the relevance of Dewey's vision for contemporary society.[12]

Both the sociable and problem-solving models of conversation empha-size the equality of conversational partners. Inside the conversation, equal-ity, civility, and fairness reign. But the barriers to entry differ. The sociable model emphasizes cultivation and sensibility; conversational partners should develop subtle capacities for fresh, entertaining, and responsive talk. The problem-solving model, in contrast, focuses on argument, the conversational partners' capacity to formulate and respond to declarative views of what the world is and what it should be like. The sociable model sees conversation as an end-in-itself, an aesthetic pleasure. The problem-solving model sees conversation as a means to the end of good government. More strongly, it pictures conversation itself as a model of good government. The skill or capacity of a competent participant in sociable conversation is verbal facility, wit, and sociability itself. The capacity of the participant in problem-solving conversation is reasonable-ness – as political theorist William Galston puts it, it is both "the willing-ness to listen seriously to a range of views" and "the willingness to set forth one's own views intelligibly and candidly as the basis of a politics of persuasion."[13]

The recuperative and interactive nature of conversation makes it par-ticularly apt as a model both of sociability on the one hand and of public reasoning on the other. So does its essentially cooperative character. Even in an argument, there is mutual support – if only in the agreement to stay engaged, to keep focused on the other person, and to not abandon the talk for either sticks and stones, on the one hand, or "the silent treatment" on the other. Even in a hostile exchange, philosopher Paul Grice's "Coopera-tive Principle" is often satisfied: that participants speak according to "the accepted purpose and direction of the talk exchange" in which they are engaged.[14]

In the sociable conversation, talk's interactive engagement provides the quality of a rich game – say, chess – with plenty of constraints on moves, but with little predictability of outcome. Likewise, the communicative virtue of problem-solving conversation is not the speaking or the listening or even their close proximity. It is the interaction of the participants and the on-going capacity for each statement to be revised in accord with the prompts or responses of the other.

This, in turn, depends on a degree of good will. An argument out of control is a conversation where each statement's ambiguity is read in the most hostile way possible. If a husband and wife are fighting, and one says, "I can't take this any more, I'm going out," the other may reply, "So you don't love me any more? You want a divorce? You're leaving me?" It might have been just as logical to respond, "Okay, maybe we both need to cool off for awhile." Just because people are in a conversation, there is no guarantee that they will take advantage of conversation's recuperative powers. Not the fact of conversation but the norms that govern it make it serviceable for democratic self-government.

There is many a slip 'twixt conversation and democratic government. Because that is so, the ground rules of conversation are more important than the spontaneity that may arise therein. Conversation can be and – without appropriate training, education, and social equality – normally is highly inegalitarian. The rules of democratic conversation can help protect the slow-of-speech, who are otherwise disenfranchised by the articulate and by the glib.

In the 1970s, political scientist Jane Mansbridge studied the famous New England town meetings. She found that, for many people, the prospect of speaking at the town meeting caused so much anxiety that they simply chose not to attend. As one Vermont farmer told her, "it does take a little bit of courage. 'Specially if you get up and make a boo-boo. I mean you make a mistake and say something, then people would never get up and say anything again. They feel themselves inferior." Florence Johnson, a house cleaner and mother of five, had never attended the town meeting when Mansbridge spoke to her: "If you go there and you speak up, they make fun of you for speaking up and so on, and I guess people just don't want to go and be made fun of." Others felt they would speak at the town meeting, but only if they got mad. A retired businessman said, "Some people are eloquent and can make others feel inferior. They can shut them down. I wouldn't say a word at town meetings unless they got me madder'n hell."

Again and again, Mansbridge found great tension arising in the town meeting or, for some citizens, at the very thought of it. Farmer Jamie Pedley got a splitting headache; an older man feared for his heart. Over and over, townspeople reported that people didn't speak up at the town meeting because of fear of criticism or fear of ridicule. Even for those who overcame their fears and attended town meetings, a willingness to speak up was very unevenly distributed. The distribution reproduced and even accentuated social inequalities. For instance, women made up 49 percent of those who attended the three meetings Mansbridge analyzed in detail, but they accounted for only 29 percent of the speakers at those meetings. When women spoke they tended to give reports or ask questions. They provided only 8 percent of "major statements of opinions" and they initiated none of the ten debates.[15]

The fear of embarrassment the Vermonters express is a fundamental human characteristic. Charles Darwin argued that every human expression of emotion except one has an analogue in other species. The distinctively human manifestation of emotion is blushing; Darwin explains that "It is not the simple act of reflecting on our own appearance, but the thinking what others think of us, which excites a blush." For sociologist Erving Goffman, the effort to avoid embarrassments provides the central and continuous drama to human social life. It is no accident that the situations Goffman regularly analyzed are public ones. There are situations where the possibility of embarrassment is minimized, particularly where people feel completely at home or where religious or political fervor or the passion of love or other intense emotions make people practically asocial, that is, relatively insensitive to the opinions of mere acquaintances or strangers. But in public meetings, street-corner conversations, and other interaction with acquaintances in public, the presentation of self and the embarrassment risked by it come to the fore.[16]

We should perhaps distinguish two kinds of conversations in democracies, both of them necessary – but in radically different ways – to the functioning of democratic society. In homogeneous conversation, people talk primarily with others who share their values and they expect that conversation will reinforce them in the views they already share. In these conversations, people may test their opinions, to be sure, and venture ideas that may not be warmly received, but they do so in full knowledge that they agree on fundamentals and that the assumptions that they share will make such experimentation safe. People may be prepared in these familial conversations for citizenship in the more daunting form of heterogeneous conversation. Here, in what we might term "truly public" conversation, citizens talk with other citizens who may not share their views and values. In these conversations, friendly testing is all but impossible; in these settings, there are penalties for expressing uncertainty and doubt, rewards for speaking with conviction and certainty. Tempers may flare and working partnerships may be frayed or severed. But there may also be the exhilaration of achieving agreement (or, for one side or another, of extracting concessions) and, in the face of the hurdle of heterogeneity, getting the public business done.[17]

It is especially in the truly public conversation that norms of reasonableness are most often invoked. Stephen Macedo, for instance, argues that opinion in a democracy is obliged to have "a certain form and quality of reasoning" if it is to have public force. At a minimum, "citizens must have public reasons and arguments to support their political actions. These public reasons should be further disciplined by contact with the reasonable and defensible aspects of our constitution and legal tradition."[18] Macedo is intent to show that liberalism is compatible with a relatively strong notion of citizenship, that is, one that asserts certain virtues or practices as a requirement of citizenship: "Citizens should participate in the spirit of public justification: not simply asserting their own positions, but considering and addressing the reasonable arguments of others, including those of public officials." Liberalism, as Macedo puts it, stands not only for toleration, law-governed liberty, and a notion of justice centered on rights but also for "reasoned self-government." The latter insists that we treat one another reasonably and meet objections "with reasons" – it is an "aspiration to public reasonableness."[19]

Macedo's view is distinguishable from both the sociable and problem-solving models of conversation I have outlined. Unlike the sociable view, it is almost ponderously solemn, earnestly envisioning a conversation oriented to the highest common ends and operating by the most rigorous norms of public morality. Aesthetics, play, and wit do not enter in. At the same time, this view is distinguishable from any model that places great emphasis on the spontaneity of conversation. Macedo's imagined conversation is not spontaneous, voluble, ever-flowing. It is hard-won. Its virtues lie as much in the preparation for conversation as in anything that might spontaneously arise within it or, certainly, anything that might be consummated within discussion itself.

This is also true in legal theorist Bruce Ackerman. Ackerman holds that "dialogue" is "the first obligation of citizenship."[20] Ackerman implies, correctly in my view, that liberalism is not founded on a "liberal subject," that is, a rational autonomous individual committed to scientific rationality and hence implicated in white male middle-class morality. Liberalism is the system designed to accommodate socially constituted persons, indeed, persons who in a sense socially construct themselves, people who take on different roles, who are different "subjects" and different selves in different situations. In public political settings, these persons leave behind or actively repress certain parts of themselves. They do not fit liberalism because they are constructed to fit it; they fit it because they are committed to making it work.

The norms of reasonableness like those Macedo envisions are not incorporated into just any conversation. Think of Grice's rules for conversation that Habermas adopts in his pragmatics of conversation. These are rules of cooperation rather than rules of reasonableness. They require less a logical relatedness in talk than a degree of social engagement, a willingness – for the time being – to subordinate any personal agenda to the continuation of the talk itself as the going concern. Talk, as Erving Goffman writes, "is an example of that arrangement by which individuals come together and sustain matters having a ratified, joint, current, and running claim upon attention, a claim which lodges them together in some sort of intersubjective, mental world."[21] That is conversation defined in a very encompassing fashion, but it does not specify conditions sufficient for the conversation that democratic theorists endorse.

Many successfully cooperative conversations fall short of a democratic ideal. Harold Pinter, in a brief play entitled *A Slight Ache*, reports on a breakfast table conversation between Flora and Edward. Edward, as we might expect, is reading the paper as the scene opens, but Flora manages to engage him in conversation:

Flora:	Have you noticed the honeysuckle this morning?
Edward:	The what?
Flora:	The honeysuckle.
Edward:	Honeysuckle? Where?
Flora:	By the back gate, Edward.
Edward:	Is that honeysuckle? I though it was . . . convolvulus, or something.
Flora:	But you know it's honeysuckle.
Edward:	I tell you I thought it was convolvulus.
(Pause.)	
Flora:	It's in wonderful flower.
Edward:	I must look.
Flora:	The whole garden's in flower this morning. The clematis. The convolvulus. Everything. I was out at seven. I stood by the pool.
Edward:	Did you say – that the convolvulus was in flower?
Flora:	Yes.
Edward:	But good God, you just denied there was any.
Flora:	I was talking about the honeysuckle.
Edward:	About the what?
Flora:	(calmly) Edward – you know that shrub outside the toolshed . . .
Edward:	Yes, yes.
Flora:	That's convolvulus.
Edward:	That?
Flora:	Yes.
Edward:	Oh. (Pause) I thought it was japonica.
Flora:	Oh, good Lord no.
Edward:	Pass the teapot, please.[22]

Funny as this is, it has all the standard-issue features of conversation. It has mutual engagement. It is an even-handed, egalitarian, turn-taking exchange. It has the give-and-take that enable repair or recuperation to take place. It has the power of transmitting information and clarifying the common world. But it does not have public reasonableness.

Public reasonableness is required where personal composure is put at risk. Of course, conversation is important in comfortable settings where we can come to know what we believe by "thinking out loud." But it is also important in uncomfortable settings where we risk embarrassment if we do not know or cannot articulate what we believe. Indeed, uncomfortable settings predominate in the institutions of public discussion. Democracy is deeply uncomfortable. It is precisely in public democratic settings that the squirmingly anxious Goffmanesque world takes hold.

The subject of conversation

Now, what is the subject of problem-solving public conversation in a democracy? The substance of conversation is taken to be nearly irrelevant in the sociable model – except that it should never be about matters serious enough to disrupt sociability. The problem-solving model is more ambitious – and more conflicted. It insists on a degree of sociability or, at least, civility but also on the capacity of the conversation to translate the sociable into the public. This also translates the public into the sociable. Democratic conversation is in part dependent on, parasitic on, the prior existence of a public world – often available in print. This reinforces the view expressed a century ago by the French sociologist Gabriel Tarde that books and newspapers provide the nearly universal substance of private conversations. Not that everyone need read the newspapers, but even those who fail to "are forced to follow the groove of their borrowed thoughts. One pen suffices to set off a million tongues."[23] Before print, Tarde suggests, conversations varied greatly from one place to another and had in common only their monotony. But with books and, especially, the press, conversations become "uniform in space and diversified in time. Every morning the papers give their publics the conversations for the day. One can be almost certain at any moment of the subject of conversation between men talking at a club, in a smoking room, in a lobby."[24] The newspaper, Tarde adds, "began as only a prolonged echo of chats and correspondences and ended up as their almost exclusive source."[25] Democratic talk centers on public matters. This also means, I believe, that what democratic conversations are *about* comes from public sources. The newspaper is the historically central source of democratic conversation – the newspaper, the laws, the public world.

Much thinking about the mass media today assumes that face-to-face conversation is a superior form of human interaction for which mass communication is a forever flawed substitute. As John Dewey wrote in 1927, "the winged words of conversation in immediate intercourse have a vital import lacking in the fixed and frozen words of written speech." Dewey acknowledged that print was necessary, a "precondition of the creation of a true public." Even so, "it and its results are but tools after all. Their final actuality is accomplished in face-to-face relationships by means of direct give and take."[26]

This tries to save the superiority of conversation over mass communication, but I do not think it succeeds. Democratic talk, after all, is often just the reverse of what Dewey (and Carey after him) suggests: face-to-face conversation leads up to something written rather than print culminating in something conversational. The consummation of democratic talk may be a signed petition, a posted notice, a written law, a written judicial opinion, a written executive order. Democracies put great store in the power of writing to secure, verify, and make public. Democracies require public memories; writing greatly enhances the capacity of public memory. So talk in democracy is civil, public, and oriented to the explicit, available, transferable communications found in print and broadcasting rather than face-to-face conversation.

Conversation at large is the DNA or germ plasm of social life. It has the capacity to replicate, to combine, to exceed itself. It is inherently neither public nor private but social. It exists not only in democracies. Conversation in democracy may differ from conversation elsewhere not because democracy bubbles up from conversation but because democratic political norms and institutions instruct and shape conversations to begin with. Nothing in conversation itself necessarily suggests democracy, not even its formal egalitarianism; in early modern Europe, it suggested, if anything, aristocracy, because it depended on cultivation.

It may be that democracy sets up norms that affect even familial or homogeneous conversations within it. Citizenship seeps from the common political forum into private settings. Where this happens, in the family, for instance, it becomes difficult for the parent to answer the child's "Why should I?" with "Because I said so." The norm of reason-giving competes with the assumption of parental authority. Democracy creates democratic conversation more than conversation naturally creates democracy. As philosopher George Kateb has suggested, democracy cultivates a certain kind of self, subtly, incompletely, but effectively nonetheless. The "mere status of citizen," he writes, which makes a person eligible to run for office or to vote, "is a continuous incitement to claim the status of citizen . . . in all nonpolitical relations of life. Indeed, the incitement is to politicize the nonpolitical relations of life and thus to democratize them."[27]

Democratic conversation presumes not so much equality and spontaneity as a normative order that insists on equality, and a social order that insists on a certain level of public-ness in talk. That is, democratic conversation is conversation not among intimates nor among strangers but among citizens who are acquainted by virtue of their citizenship. Strangers will miscommunicate because they do not share background knowledge and commitment to common norms; intimates will communicate without speaking, without stating their premises, without raising potential conflicts and embarrassments. Democratic conversation, in contrast to both, is a facility of public communication under norms of public reasonableness, not simply a facility of social interaction.

Sociable talk takes place among social equals, not necessarily intimates, in clubs and coffee houses. Where democratic conversation takes place is more difficult to pin down. It may take place in discussion of values among intimates in a family. But the fully public democratic conversation takes place, as I have suggested, in settings where talk is bound to be uncomfortable. This is a kind of talk people are particularly loath to engage in – it invites conflict, and whether it is in small-town Vermont or elsewhere, people prefer sociable conversation to potentially explosive conversation.[28] Such talk is threatening enough to require formal or informal rules of engagement. Look, for instance, at the rules established for talk at the Constitutional convention, the "Ur-conversation" of the United States.

On Friday, May 25, 1787, the Constitutional convention met for the first time. Its opening business was promptly taken care of – George Washington was selected president of the convention, and a committee was appointed to prepare rules of procedure. Its proposed rules included that, when one member of the meeting held the floor, other members should not talk with one another "or read a book, pamphlet or paper, printed or manuscript." No one could speak more than twice on the same question without special permission and could speak the second time only if all others who wanted to speak had had a chance to do so. These rules of equal respect and equal opportunity for participation were supplemented with rules to encourage deliberate consideration of issues, rules for public reasonableness. A complicated question could be divided at the request of any member. Any state could have a vote postponed until the next day even if debate was concluded. Any written document to be considered was to be read through once for information and then debated by paragraphs. Rules of civility were also proposed. Any member could be called to order by any other member and would then "be allowed to explain his conduct or expressions, supposed to be reprehensible." The president would decide questions of order without appeal or debate.

All the committee's proposed rules met with general approval – except one: there was objection to the proposal that any member could call for yeas and nays and have them entered into the minutes. The acts of the

Convention did not bind the delegates' constituents in any way, Rufus King of Massachusetts reminded the Convention, and so it was unnecessary to show the votes to them. George Mason added that keeping a written record of the votes would prejudice members against changing their votes even when their convictions changed. An astute social psychologist, Mason suggested that recording votes would force people toward self-consistency even when reason led them to change their minds. Besides, Mason added, the record would then be a weapon in the hands of adversaries of the results of the Convention. These objections won the day.

All of this suggests, I think, that what makes conversation democratic is not free, equal, and spontaneous expression but equal access to the floor, equal participation in setting the ground rules for discussion, and a set of ground rules designed to encourage pertinent speaking, attentive listening, appropriate simplifications, and widely apportioned speaking rights. The primal American political conversation was carefully structured so that – within the eighteenth-century limits of who counted as a citizen – it could be genuinely deliberative and genuinely democratic. It thus had to be anything but spontaneous.

Conclusion: conversation in democracy

Conversation provides no magic solution to problems of democracy. Democracy has little to do with intimacy and little to do with community. It can be thrilling, it can be boring, it can provoke anxiety, it is often uncomfortable. I rarely enjoy the deliberative discourse of publics assembled in relatively large numbers to make decisions. I prefer two-person conversations to large gatherings. I prefer seminars to large assemblies. The larger the group, the more I want rules of engagement because I am slow of speech. This is part of what the romance-of-conversation fails to understand.

There is another thing I would add, as a coda, that the romance-of-conversation fails to grasp. Democracy sometimes requires withdrawal from conversation, withdrawal from common public subjects. Democracy, as Stephen Holmes suggests, may insist that even talk itself be constrained.[29] In the United States, the dangers of disunion and dismemberment of state and civil society by religious passions led to the First Amendment and now a 200-year history of specific Constitutional efforts to keep religion out of political discussion. Democracy may, in a sense, choose to gag its political deliberations, removing them to civil society or the private sphere. Democracies may even choose to gag directly political speech in the interests of fair-minded deliberation. The most familiar instance of this, practiced throughout the United States, is a prohibition on political speech within a certain specified distance of polling places on election day. Here speech is treated as action, as a form of intimidation or unfair advantage. Legislators around the country have concluded that a moat of political silence should surround the castle of the polling place. In voters' last steps toward the voting booth, collective rights of political expression are sacrificed to individual rights of personal deliberation.

Important as civil, rule-governed conversation is to democracy, democracy may sometimes require withdrawal from civility itself. Democracy may sometimes require that your interlocutor does not wait politely for you to finish but shakes you by the collar and cries "Listen! Listen for God's sake!" We call these situations social movements, strikes, demonstrations. We call the people who initiate such departures from civility driven, ambitious, unreasonable, self-serving, rude, hot-headed, self-absorbed. The likes of Newt Gingrich and Martin Luther King Jr. and William Lloyd Garrison. All of these are people willing to engage in democratic conversation but also pugnacious beyond the point of civility, even willing to make their case to opt out of conversation altogether, at least temporarily and strategically. Any full-bodied concept of democracy and the place of conversation in it would have to take account of the instances where conversation is itself an impediment to democracy's fulfillment.

10

The trouble with experts –
and why democracies need them

For many thinkers, expertise is a permanent embarrassment to democratic theory. For both theoretical and historical reasons, a variety of critics committed to democratic values and democratic institutions distrust experts. There are few terms in American political discourse that speak more praise than "grass roots" or sneer more convincingly than "elitist." Nevertheless, I intend to argue here that democrats should adopt a more forgiving view of the role of expertise in a democracy.

The trouble with experts

The view I challenge is that "the relation between democracy and expert knowledge is troubled," as James March and Johan Olsen gently put it, that granting political authority to experts or deferring to their authority is inconsistent with democracy.[1] This position took on a classic form in US political thought in 1927 in John Dewey's rejoinder to the work of Walter Lippmann. In the years following World War I, Lippmann despaired about democracy. He pointed to the incapacity of ordinary men and women to command enough accurate information about the world to govern themselves adequately. In *Public Opinion* (1922), Lippmann argued that ordinary citizens do not perceive the world directly but only through the set of forms and stereotypes provided by the press. People could still comprehend directly their immediate environment, but they saw the wider world that impinged on their lives only through a media-constructed "pseudo-environment." Journalism could improve and bring its picture of the outside world closer to reality – but it could not, in Lippmann's view, improve very much. The press provided news accurately only when journalists could depend on an efficient "machinery of record." When other institutions provided reliable baseball scores or stock market quotations, journalists transmitted solid information to the public. When such materials were not available, journalists could not be trusted to do very good work. News and truth are different, Lippmann argues. News picks out from the wide world only what its imperfect "searchlight" reveals, and the searchlight is guided by market forces, political wishes, and cognitive blind spots, not by any kind of scientific aspiration to truth. Lippmann urged the establishment of "political observatories", what we now call "think tanks," to conduct scientific studies and monitor politics in the many ways journalists themselves could not.[2] If journalists had experts to rely on, they could inform the citizenry responsibly. Experts – people who cultivated the habit of discounting their own expectations, as Lippmann put it (that is, people who tried to put aside their own interests and wishes when they examined the world) – were the best hope to save democracy from itself. Lippmann did not propose that experts run the government but that the elected officials who run the government call on experts.

John Dewey agreed with Lippmann that the general public has very little understanding of the political world – and very little interest in it. "In most circles," Dewey wrote, "it is hard work to sustain conversation on a political theme; and once initiated, it is quickly dismissed with a yawn."[3] But Dewey was more reluctant than Lippmann to concede disinterest to experts. For him, experts, like any class of rulers, ultimately speak for their own private interests rather than for the public interest. They will become an oligarchy so long as "the masses do not have the chance to inform the experts as to their needs." This does not mean, for Dewey, that experts should not be empowered, only that communication between experts and the public is essential. "Inquiry, indeed, is a work which devolves upon experts," Dewey acknowledged. The experts would not be responsible for "framing and executing policies" but for "discovering and making known the facts upon which the former depend."[4] Of course, separating fact-finding from policy-making is much easier said than done.

The Lippmann/Dewey exchange is preface to a much more thoroughgoing attack on expertise in the 1960s and after. Many social critics at that point attacked the authority of experts, as did New Left activists generally. The debunking of professional authority had roots in Marx, Nietzsche, and Freud, but it reached a high point in the egalitarian fervor that spread from the civil rights movement to the women's movement to academic life and the professions themselves in the sixties. In the field of sociology, it had a somewhat distinctive history, with a subfield known as the "sociology of knowledge" having insisted, even before the sixties, that what passes as authoritative knowledge in society is "socially constructed," subject to the play of power and the occupational self-interest of groups that produce or use knowledge. The sociology of knowledge became conventional wisdom inside sociology, exemplified in Everett Hughes' remark that, in sociological terms, a "quack" is simply a professional who agrees with his customers more than with his colleagues.[5] But only in the 1960s did the sociology of knowledge, or something like it, become part of an energetic and aggressive public discussion, and largely through the efforts of non-sociologists.

This discussion had many sources, but it was actively advanced in many fields by a brilliant, short, and accessible, or seemingly accessible, book in the history of the physical sciences by Thomas Kuhn, published in 1962, *The Structure of Scientific Revolutions*. Kuhn suggested that the development of science was not a progressive accumulation of new knowledge explained by better and better theories but that it was a tumultuous movement from one state to another, each state operating inside a "paradigm" or set of theoretical presumptions incommensurate with other paradigms. When a given paradigm could no longer manage to explain a growing set of puzzles and when younger scientists came along with a new paradigm that handled the puzzles, science would shift into a new gear defined by the new paradigm. Kuhn called this a scientific revolution. And while it could be defined in intellectual terms – the capacity of a new theoretical structure to incorporate an explanation of certain factual anomalies that the old theoretical structure failed at – Kuhn made it clear that this was a social as much as a cognitive revolution. The new paradigm gained command, after all, not from the blinding power of its ideas but from the fact that older scientists, committed to the older paradigm, eventually retired or died. Kuhn cites with approval the remark of the physicist Max Planck that "a new scientific truth does not triumph by convincing its opponents and making them see the light, but rather because its opponents eventually die, and a new generation grows up that is familiar with it."[6]

Directly inspired by Kuhn's work in some cases, but in every case responding to the broad cultural revolt against authority of the 1960s, studies of law, medicine, psychiatry, sociology, organized knowledge in general, and professionals and experts at large pointed to the inevitable complicity of knowledge and power.[7] This position that so many studies, polemics, and outraged essays articulated in the 1960s and 1970s would be summarized later with enduring force by Michel Foucault's term "power/knowledge." The term insists not that politics corrupts knowledge but that power and knowledge are two sides of the same coin, they interpenetrate, they do not exist independently of each other. Foucault distinguishes his position from critiques of ideology because any notion of ideology implicitly or explicitly contrasts "ideology" to "truth." The problem is with the notion of "truth." For Foucault, the task is to see historically "how effects of truth are produced within discourses which in themselves are neither true nor false."[8] For Foucault, truth is not innocent and opposed to the corrupt category of power but is itself:

> a thing of this world: it is produced only by virtue of multiple forms of constraint. And it induces regular effects of power. Each society has its regime of truth, its "general politics" of truth: that is, the types of discourse which it accepts and makes function as true; the mechanisms and instances which enable one to distinguish true and false statements, the means by which each is sanctioned; the techniques and procedures accorded value in the acquisition of truth; the status of those who are charged with saying what counts as true.[9]

That power and knowledge are intertwined is not a corruption of true knowledge, but the very nature of knowledge, everywhere and always.

These works and others make the case against experts a great deal more severe than in Dewey's writing half a century earlier. Dewey, after all, accepted the neutrality of experts' knowledge and distrusted only the lack of experts' democratic accountability when decision-making was turned over to them. The premise of contemporary work is that the knowledge that experts produce is itself situated, that there is no such thing as neutral knowledge – in a sense, that there is scarcely anything one might recognize as genuinely "technical" knowledge.[10] As Stephen P. Turner summarizes current views of science in the cultural studies literature, there are two separable charges against science and expertise from the vantage of democracy. First, the very notion of expertise violates the rough equality among citizens that is presupposed by the idea of democracy. If there is such a thing as expertise and if expertise touches on matters relevant to policy decisions in a democracy, then some people (experts) have more relevant information than others to bring to the table and this gives their voices disproportionate weight. Second, and this is what more recent criticism adds to Dewey, if expertise is invariably contingent or conditional, then there can be nothing neutral about the expert's purported neutrality, least of all the claim to neutrality itself.[11]

A moderate critique of expertise

In relation to this array of critical work, a political theorist like Ian Shapiro sounds very cautious indeed when he suggests that it is acceptable for people to defer to expertise in a variety of circumstances. For Shapiro, it is okay to believe Einstein's theory of relativity to be true even without understanding it: "In certain (although not all) circumstances one can reasonably act on the advice of an airplane pilot, an auto mechanic, an architect, or a physician without understanding its rationale or even being interested in it. But the idea that there is analogous political expertise reasonably prompts suspicion."[12] What is reasonable about suspicions concerning political expertise? For Shapiro, the most important objection to political expertise is: "The experts always turn out to be on somebody's side, and not necessarily ours."[13] This echoes Dewey but with a tincture of Foucault. Shapiro believes there is such a thing as technical knowledge; even so, he does not seem to hold that knowledge and power are ultimately separable.

This does prompt suspicion – but should it? Is the technical expertise of the pilot or mechanic so thoroughly distinct from the policy knowledge of the economist, political scientist, think-tank policy wonk, State Department country specialist, or OMB analyst? I think the expertise of the pilot, mechanic, architect, or physician is not as purely technical as Shapiro may assume and the expertise of the policy-relevant experts is not as difficult to separate from value judgments and political preferences as he imagines.

Let me take the first part of this first. Consider the expertise of the car mechanic. As anyone who listens to National Public Radio's *Car Talk* knows, the diagnosis of the car's problem is strictly separated from values, but the remedy the mechanic proposes does not follow unerringly from the diagnosis. The proposed remedy often has as much to do with the car's owner as the car. In some cases, the mechanic will be able to say, regardless of the character of the driver, "do not drive that car anywhere except to the closest garage, it's a disaster waiting to happen!" But, more often, the mechanic has a wide range of discretion in recommending action. The mechanic may ask about who drives the car regularly, what kind of driver or drivers they are, what kind of driving (city or country, long or short hauls) they normally undertake, how long they hope to keep the car, whether they want to maintain the car to pass on to a teenage son or daughter, and how wealthy they are. Decisions about repair are economic and social as well as technical. An alert consumer will be able to distinguish between the mechanic's diagnosis and the mechanic's recommended remedy, but most consumers are seeking not only professional acuity in diagnosis but professional judgment in advice.

Granted, not all types of expertise are in this respect identical. People turn to architects, for instance, as they do to car mechanics, for expertise that blends technical knowledge with general understanding of how human beings of different sorts and at different life stages live in and respond to their physical environments. When people turn to heart surgeons or airline pilots, in contrast, they place greater weight on specifically technical knowledge. If a surgeon's technical skill is reputed to be impeccable, a grating bedside manner or an authoritarian, impatient style of decision-making is forgiven.

Shapiro concedes that at least economists really do have some esoteric knowledge, relatively pure technical knowledge relevant to governance. What is vital is that their counsel should be advice, not authoritative decision-making. They may deserve special attention but "economic policy-making should never be ceded to professional economists."[14] In this remark, Shapiro reverts to Dewey and jettisons Foucault. In Turner's useful distinction, Shapiro is finally concerned about the problem of equality, not the problem of neutrality.

This, for Shapiro, is the crucial point, whether it is the role of economists in economic policy-making or the role of psychiatrists and finger-print experts in criminal trials: "The intelligent democratic use of expertise subordinates it to lay control through institutional devices, like the jury, that are designed to limit its imperialistic tendencies without stifling its esoteric content."[15] But to agree that expert knowledge should be subordinated to lay control is just the beginning of the problem of expertise in democracy. Take the very example Shapiro offers – the jury. There are serious proposals that in certain kinds of complex cases, juries comprised of untutored representatives of the general community are an inadequate institutional mechanism for decision-making. Some states, in fact, have provision for "special juries" where some further qualification – usually an educational qualification – is instituted. In federal courts, the Jury Selection and Service Act of 1968 terminated elite or special juries as violating civil rights, but special juries persisted in state courts.[16] In some highly technical domains like patent infringement cases, judges have found ways to limit the jury's autonomy. In other instances, alternative means of adjudication place authority in the hands of experts appointed as "trustees" or "special masters," particularly in allocating monetary awards to parties in mass tort claims if litigation persists.[17]

Even with standard juries, jurors are not as supreme in practice as they are in theory. The jury is not free to deliberate on any question it chooses but on the questions the judge presents to it and in the way the judge frames them. The experts who testify in a trial are submitting their expertise to the judgment of democratic decision-makers, but it is a double submission – to the jury, on the one hand, and to the elected or appointed judge, on the other. The judge and the jury operate in tandem and the judge ordinarily has considerable influence over how the jury will conduct itself. In particular, the judge controls what testimony the jury will be permitted to hear. Interestingly, this may make jury trials more fair than judge-adjudicated trials because judges, like all other human beings, have a limited capacity to disregard information that they have heard even if they declare it to be legally inadmissible. In a jury trial, in contrast, the judge as expert manager of the proceedings, is ordinarily able to prevent the jury from hearing inadmissible evidence. The capacity of the jury to come to sound judgment is thus constructed in part by the expertise of the judge.[18]

Of course, not all expert opinions in policy-making are submitted to a jury. Most democracies do not employ juries at all, and even in Britain, where juries originated, less than 1 percent of civil trials go to a jury, and even in criminal trials the figure is just 2 percent.[19] The United States is exceptional in its use of juries.[20] (It may also be true that Americans are more likely than others to find it difficult to reconcile expertise and democracy.) But what about other situations where expertise has a prominent role in policy-making? For instance, what makes juries relevant in criminal trials but keeps the Federal Reserve's decisions about setting interest rates from being submitted to a jury? Have we made an error, as far as preserving democracy is concerned, to cede so much authority to Alan Greenspan (or his successor as Federal Reserve chair, Ben Bernanke)? Should Greenspan have been required to make a case to a jury to raise or lower interest rates? If so, should the jury have decided on the basis of the preponderance of the evidence? Or on the presence or absence of reasonable doubt? Should the presumption have been for or against Greenspan's proposals? How would the fiscal jury be instructed – and by whom? The Federal Reserve is about as close to a situation of pure expert policy-making as the United States has. Even it, however, is subject to democratic control. The 7 members of the Board of Governors are appointed to 14-year terms by the President with the consent of the Senate. From this group of 7, the President selects, with the consent of the Senate, a chairman for a 4-year term. Would this satisfy Dewey? Would it satisfy Shapiro? Or are 14-year terms too long? Or should there be term limits for the chair? It is impossible to answer these questions for Dewey or Shapiro because neither addresses the tedious, but vital, matter of the length of the leash on which democracy places the expert.

The length of the leash

Shapiro's objection to expertise in politics, like Dewey's, is in the end unpersuasive because it is too distant from actual political practice. Every governmental use of expertise is ultimately under the control of democratic authorities, even if the experts may sometimes be on a long leash. The length of the leash, not the relevance of experts, is frequently the matter at issue. Actual problems about expertise in democracy are generally of two sorts. First, what are the best institutional mechanisms for keeping experts responsible to the people's representatives – while still enabling their expertise to bear on and improve decision-making? In other words, how can the leash be short enough to provide accountability and preserve democracy? Second, there is the other side of the coin: how does democratic authority give experts enough autonomy so that the voice of the expert represents the expert's expertise rather than the views of politicians or bureaucrats who pressure the expert into submission? In other words, how can the leash be long enough to keep the expert from becoming a toady?

In practice, the latter problem is usually the more serious one. There are certainly cases outside democracies where experts have behaved inhumanly, allowing loyalty to a regime to supersede loyalty to professional ethics and professional oaths. The extreme case is summed up in the title of a study by Robert Jay Lifton – *The Nazi Doctors*.[21] The doctors who conducted experiments on concentration camp prisoners were obviously not true to their oath as physicians to "first do no harm." Are there similar, if less extreme, instances in democracies?

Certainly there are. In fact, Lifton himself has written about one of them: he has called on physicians in the US military services who might have knowledge of the abuses of prisoners at Abu Ghraib prison in Iraq or knowledge of other uses of torture by American military personnel to speak out about it.[22] Steven Miles, at the Center for Bioethics at the University of Minnesota, has gone further to accuse US military medical personnel of "complicity" with abuses of prisoners in Iraq, Afghanistan, and Guantanamo Bay, and to call for an inquiry. There is evidence that medical reports on detainees, including death certificates, were falsified or their completion delayed. Knowledge of torture at Abu Ghraib was widespread in the military, including among medical personnel, but no medical officer reported the abuses. The role of physicians and other medical personnel deserves special attention, Miles argues, "because of the moral obligations of medical professionals with regard to torture and because of horror at health professionals who are silently or actively complicit with torture."[23]

Here, as in most cases where experts in positions of authority fail in their obligations, the professionals abandon loyalty to their professionalism to serve the requirements of bureaucracies or state (and elected) power. People have certainly questioned whether the expertise of the Central Intelligence Agency is genuinely expert – for instance, do agents have enough training and experience to know when their sources are reliable and when they are not? But the larger complaint with the performance of the CIA does not question technical expertise but the willingness of intelligence professionals to stand by their professionalism. The concern is that "group-think" pressures inside the organization prevent experts from reporting their views fully and accurately and that officials at the top of the agency misrepresent its knowledge to elected leaders to give them the advice they want to hear. The problem is not that experts have too much authority but that they have too little. Their expertise may be dangerous, not from its imperialism but from its fragility, crumbling before the power of bureaucracy or politics.

David Halberstam's classic study of American policy-making in Vietnam has this flavor, although it is routinely misinterpreted as a critique of experts. Halberstam's title, *The Best and the Brightest*, refers not to experts but to a self-confident, quasi-aristocratic corps of tough-minded men whose unyielding arrogance derived not from professional training or expertise but from class rearing, from the Kennedy administration's fetishistic embrace of swagger and style, and from the sway of office itself where, as heads of departments and agencies, they could ignore or silence subordinates. They were not professionals with credentials, technical training, or long experience, nor were they answerable to professional peers. In fact, Halberstam's own sympathies lie again and again with genuine experts, the well-informed State Department officers whose cautions were repeatedly ignored by the political appointees from this privileged group. Halberstam takes to task Secretary of Defense Robert McNamara for ignoring critical reports by State Department experts, Secretary of State Dean Rusk for ignoring the experienced hands in his own department, and General Richard Stilwell, among other military commanders, for castigating Halberstam's own *New York Times* reports, later to be confirmed as true.[24]

What exactly is an expert? An expert is someone in possession of specialized knowledge that is accepted by the wider society as legitimate. An expert's knowledge includes specific, technical skill based on some wider appreciation of the field of knowledge in question. In academic areas, we say that someone "knows the literature," that is, knows the debates and the questions relevant to the use of the specialized knowledge at hand. The expert's knowledge is rooted in a body of knowledge sufficiently well codified to be passed on through formal training. Expertise grows as well, over time, from clinical experience.

It should be obvious that the expert's knowledge, so defined, is socially compromised or socially constructed – it is not knowledge directly of the world but knowledge of a lore collectively claimed by an expert or professional group. How could it be otherwise? What defines an expert as a sociological type is willingness to submit to the authority of a group of peers. What enabled the rise of the practice of academic freedom, as historian Thomas Haskell analyzes it, is the emergence of professional communities that provided an alternative source of authority, social reference, control, and identity to scholars whose paychecks nonetheless came from a single institution. The rise of these professional communities afforded "the opportunity . . . for professors to divide their loyalties, thereby complicating their identity and enhancing their authority."[25] Professionalism is thus, for Haskell, defined by two features – first, the divided loyalty of the professional and, second, the self-governance of the professional community: "The cardinal principle of professional autonomy is collegial self-governance; its inescapable corollary is that only one's peers are competent to judge one's performance."[26]

How can democracy be organized to make optimal use of expertise? While ultimate decision-making must always belong to the political process, often that process will work best when it affords experts great autonomy. Fawning experts are not useful experts. Fearful experts are not useful experts. In practical politics, too little expertise is more problematic, and more common, than too much. If this point was obscure to democratic theorists in the past, it is much more salient today in light of what journalist Chris Mooney has called "the Republican war on science."[27] This war includes efforts of the federal government to demand certain political or ideological views of scientists appointed to scientific advisory panels, to limit the attendance of government scientists at international AIDS conferences, and to overrule expert advisory panel recommendations for partisan purposes.[28] It includes White House efforts to edit expert reports on global climate change to minimize attention to the negative impact of greenhouse gases on the environment.[29] The administration has also placed restrictions on government scientists who give public lectures or write publicly or speak on the record to reporters when those scientists disagree with the Bush administration position on global warming.[30] Some of these actions simply place short-term political objectives over the authority of scientific knowledge; some of them also suggest, in Kevin Phillips' disturbing phrase, the emergence of an "American theocracy" that rejects scientific procedures altogether if they appear to conflict with orthodox religious conviction.[31]

Why democracies need experts

When experts are serving democratic governance well, what is it that they do? Experts can provide three services:

(1)   Experts can speak truth to power. When expertise is doing its appointed task in a democracy, it is providing to decision-makers, publicly or privately, a record of truth as an alternative source of information and authority to the established view of the leader. When their counsel is made public, they model a form of authority to which, to a degree, a general public can aspire, and which a general public can use for its own decision-making purposes. What makes this possible is not wizardry. Experts do not always have the right answer. What makes it possible are: (a) methods, training, and experience that provides the expert competence in knowledge areas where most people are not competent; (b) an ethical or professional commitment to truth-seeking according to the best standards of the expert community; and (c) a willingness to be judged as qualified or unqualified by the expert community.

As Dewey and Shapiro both point out, experts, like everybody else, tend to favor themselves rather than to favor truth. The task is to minimize that danger when experts are empowered. And this can be done, in no small part by the very identity of the expert as an expert. One example may stand in for many others: economist Douglas J. Holtz-Eakin was the director of the putatively non-partisan Congressional Budget Office in 2004, a position he had held since early 2003. Before his appointment to this position, he was the chief economist for the White House Council of Economic Advisers. It is not surprising that Democrats in the Congress were skeptical about having a Bush insider running the chief economic information source for Congress. However, soon after taking office, Holtz-Eakin concluded that the Bush economic plans would not reduce the deficit and would not stimulate long-term economic growth. He acknowledged that the Bush tax plan strongly favored the wealthiest Americans. Under fire from conservative columnists (and more gentle concern from Congressional Republicans), Holtz-Eakin replied exactly as the ideal-type expert is supposed to: "The only shield one has in a job like this is your professional credibility. If you try to play games with that, you end up in a morass and won't know what to do. It's not workable."[32] Hired into a position specifically designed to serve all members of the Congress, instructed to provide the Congress his best professional judgment, no matter how uncomfortable it might be for his friends, he did exactly that. And he did not, by his own account, show unusual courage in doing so – he showed an allegiance to his professional reputation. This is exactly what experts are supposed to do, not because they are smarter than others or more virtuous, but because they are experts. They are not quacks. They desire to please their professional peers more than their clients.

(2)   Experts can clarify the grounds of public debate and so improve the capacity of both legislators and the general public to engage effectively

in democratic decision-making. They can clarify policy alternatives. They can clarify the costs and benefits of different proposed plans of action – exactly as Holtz-Eakin did. The Congressional Budget Office is an institution chartered for just that purpose.

There is a similar, if less weighty, authority in California that plays a comparable role but, instead of offering non-partisan expert advice to the legislators, it provides that advice to voters. The Office of the Legislative Analyst assesses the fiscal impact of each initiative or proposition on the California election ballot, and the analyst's conclusions are printed in the voter information pamphlet the state mails out a few weeks before an election to every registered voter in the state. The analyst does not say that the voter would be wise to vote one way or the other. The analyst simply reports what, in her best professional judgment, the fiscal consequences would be if the ballot measure succeeds.

Experts can display relevant knowledge and they can assess what relevant information is not known, or not known with assurance, or not likely to be known. To put all of this very simply, one of the things that experts do is teach. They distribute their expertise broadly. That distribution does not turn everyone into an expert but it does empower people beyond the established circle of expertise. Expertise, unlike aristocratic cultivation or divine inspiration, is a form of authority that, to a degree, can be passed on and shared. There is not enough emphasis on this in professional training but it is a critical feature of expertise in and for democracies.

On occasion, non-certified non-experts can by sheer determination pick up enough expert knowledge to become players in the expert policy game. The best documented example of this is sociologist Steven Epstein's account of how AIDS activists picked up enough medical knowledge to become instrumental in improving the scientific trials of drugs for AIDS and AIDS-related illnesses. At first, they had railed against the power of the professionals; later they decided to beat them by joining them.[33] Where Epstein praises AIDS activists for attacking the rule of experts and politicizing medical science in their efforts to promote research attention to AIDS, he criticizes the Bush administration's attacks on scientific experts. Is he therefore inconsistent? His claim is that AIDS activists "displayed enormous dedication to the task of learning mainstream science" and were "deeply invested in the scientific process," while Bush administration attacks have been little more than "an opportunistic endorsement of whatever seemed consistent with predetermined political stances."[34]

(3) Experts can diagnose opportunity and diagnose injustice. So can non-experts. But experts have the resources, especially in a legalistic culture, to do so effectively in ways that pose a policy-related question. This empowers the general public that might be perfectly capable of

discerning a problem or trouble without being qualified to translate that general trouble into a legislatively or administratively decidable issue. When people sue, they file what is called a complaint. Normally, they do this through an attorney. Attorneys are, in a sense, professional complainers. Complaining can be a very important, democratic act. Plaintiffs – those who offer the complaint – may be seeking justice against the government for its use of Agent Orange, or against the government for nuclear testing that endangered their health, or against tobacco companies, or against Swiss banks that profited from the Holocaust, or against Saudi Arabia for financing terrorism. These are all real examples where individuals alone or as part of class action suits have sought damages because expert lawyers were able to translate individual harms into legitimate, workable calls for justice.

If worse comes to worse and experts abuse their power, they are more easily dismissed than any other kind of cultural or political authority. This is true when they are hired or consulted by politicians or government agencies. It is not true when they themselves hold or very nearly hold the reins of power, as physicians may do in a hospital or academics in a university. There the self-protective power of the guild makes it difficult (although by no means impossible) to dismiss venal or incompetent members.

Politicians as experts

So far, I have spoken about experts in the most conventional sense, referring to persons with specialized knowledge, usually but not always certified by educational credentials and participation in professional communities. Before concluding, it is important to consider a special kind of expertise in democratic governance, one that elected representatives do not hire or consult but possess themselves. In democracies, there are experts who are keepers of historical memory – like historians and lawyers; there are experts in the rules of democratic procedure – lawyers and parliamentarians; there are experts in relevant databases for democratic decision-making – economists, demographers, statisticians, officials at the Bureau of the Census; there are government officials with political experience who, like auto mechanics and others with experience and well-honed clinical judgment acquired over time, merit special deference; and there are experts in political science who have knowledge of the mechanisms, good and bad, of elections, legislatures, and electoral systems.

Still, the most distinctive and important political "expert" in a democracy is the elected legislator or elected executive officer. Because elected representatives typically become professional politicians, remaining in office not only for one term but for as many terms as, within the limits of law, their constituencies will re-elect them to serve, not only do they become experts on one or more domains of public affairs but they become linked to and loyal to views and values current in the legislatures where they serve, not necessarily views and values of the constituents who elected them. The legitimacy of representation as a democratic mechanism is thus, as Ian Shapiro writes, "inescapably suspect."[35] In fact, as Bernard Manin has carefully argued, the central institution of democratic governance in ancient Greece was the selection of leaders by lottery, not by election. Election, as political theorists recognized into the eighteenth century, was a mode of selecting leaders well-designed for aristocracies, not democracies.[36]

In this regard, the politician takes on the character of expert, and the first problem of "expertise" in a democracy is whether the elected official should represent the views of constituents (leaving aside the nasty problem of how the representative is even to know what the constituents think) or should be responsible to the constituency by exercising his or her own best judgment. This is a classic problem, of course – whether the representative should be an "agent" of constituents, voting just as they would vote, or a "trustee," elected to exercise judgment. The most famous discussion of this remains Edmund Burke's speech to the voters of Bristol in 1774. Burke acknowledged that constituents' wishes:

> ought to have great weight with him; their opinion high respect; their business unremitted attention. It is his duty to sacrifice his repose, his pleasures, his satisfactions, to theirs – and above all, ever, and in all cases, to prefer their interest to his own. But his unbiased opinion, his mature judgment, his enlightened conscience, he ought not to sacrifice to you. . . . Your representative owes you, not his industry alone, but his judgment: and he betrays, instead of serving you, if he sacrifices it to your opinion.[37]

On the great majority of issues that come before legislators today, the constituency has no known or likely views at all. Legislators, according to several close observers of them at both state and federal levels, choose the Burkean trustee role over the agent role not because they are uninterested in or contemptuous of what their constituents think but because their constituents do not think anything at all on most political questions: "Legislators choose the trustee role because they regard it as the only viable one given the greater knowledge they have as a result of their involvement in the legislative process on the one hand and the paucity of constituency attention to most issues on the other."[38] It is very rare that legislators' conscience conflicts with constituency desires – the classic case that Burke calls our attention to; but it is an everyday and unavoidable occurrence that legislators must act on questions where their constituents have little interest, less knowledge, and nothing at stake. What is true of legislators is likewise true of administrators and other specialized agents of government.

Although elected representatives often become experts, they also make use of expertise by hiring experts on their staffs. The legislator does not control the staff person nor the staff person the legislator but they work together in an interaction, a dialogue. Note that staffers may not even live in a legislator's district, they may not even be citizens, but they have more of a voice in law-making than almost any voter in the district.

Staffers are not the only experts legislators depend on. Very often, legislators trust in other legislators to act as experts on particular issues. No one in a national legislature has the knowledge to judge the vast range of questions on which the legislature takes action. Legislators get by, nonetheless, by relying on colleagues, normally of their own party, who serve with them in the legislature and have special expertise or experience in other areas. Legislators seek as experts not only colleagues with technical knowledge but those with a set of priorities or values sympathetic to their own. They choose to rely on expert colleagues the same way they might choose an architect to design a home. They do not know enough to design a house themselves but they are informed enough to know which architect to trust and which architect understands and sympathizes with their aesthetic and moral preferences.

John Kingdon shows in his classic study of how members of Congress decide how to vote that representatives rely much more on other representatives than they do on outside experts for their voting decisions. They turn to other members of Congress, particularly those who are of the same party who share values and preferences. No one offers better counsel than these colleagues because, as fellow politicians, they give advice in recognition of the representative's political needs, they have public and known records themselves, and not incidentally they are "readily available at the time of voting, a consideration of paramount importance."[39] Recent studies continue to confirm that representatives in the House regularly turn to the colleagues they respect on issues where they themselves are not well informed but that this is less so in the Senate where senators rely much more on their own large staffs of expert legislative analysts.[40]

Making experts safe for democracy

In defending expertise as compatible with and complementary to democracy, and indeed ineradicable from any conceivable scheme of elective, representative government, I do not advocate releasing experts from accountability to democratic institutions. Professionalism is fraught with exactly the perils that Dewey, Shapiro, and others point to. As Thomas Haskell has observed: "In the absence of countervailing forces, it is probably true that all human organizations tend to devolve into country clubs and fraternal lodges. Unchecked, the republic of letters becomes a republic of pals. The only remedy for this degenerative tendency is for individuals deliberately to embrace values that offset and counter-balance it."[41] Haskell applauds "the community of the competent" not because it affords us a perfect solution but because "insofar as its members genuinely engage in mutual criticism and pride themselves on suspicion of professional closure, they make it, too, a partially self-correcting enterprise."[42]

In addition to the self-regulating capacities of expert communities themselves, democracies have developed a wide range of ways of incorporating experts and different lengths of leash on which experts are drawn into democratic decision-making. Sometimes the relative autonomy of the experts should be very high. In fact, for all practical purposes, the federal government cedes at least for the length of a term of office ultimate decision-making authority to experts at the National Science Foundation, the National Institutes of Health, the Securities and Exchange Commission, the Federal Reserve, and the National Endowment for the Humanities. There are other cases, as when members of Congress invite experts to testify at hearings, or when the president appoints a blue-ribbon panel to offer an assessment of a national problem, where the power of the experts may be neutralized by disagreements among them, or, even if the experts arrive at consensus, where their power is diluted greatly by their distance from actual policy-making involvement.

The objection to expertise in democracy from Dewey to the present needs to overcome its own romanticism. It fails to see not only the complexity of democracy but the democracy of complexity – in a world too complex for any one person or agency to comprehend, there is no governing without colleagues, consulting, committees, and compromise, and there is an iterative process of building consensus. Dialogue is too simple and linear a model of what democracy should be about. Arriving at agreement in a group is subtle, subject to multiple forces, evolving over time with changes and swings in mood rather than strict rational debate. Democratic cognition is and must be distributed cognition – but it need not be evenly distributed.

The best democracy does not seek to minimize the role of expertise. A democracy without experts will either fail to get things done or fail to get things done well enough to satisfy citizens. There is no good reason to judge democracy incompatible with specialization. There is no good reason to imagine democracy incompatible with what we can call functional authorization. In a university, faculty in the music department have great power in selecting faculty and graduate students in music, but little power to select faculty and graduate students in chemistry. But the chemists, likewise, have scarcely any power to select faculty and students for the music department. The decisions of either department can be reviewed or appealed in the Academic Senate or with the provost or dean. But this happens rarely. Functional authorization is how the institution operates. It is how governments work, too.

None of us is sufficiently well informed to make judgments about every important issue before the public. We all have to trust others. As Robert Dahl has observed, "This is true not only of ordinary citizens but of the most highly informed scholars and experts, who in making judgments about the truth or validity of most questions invariably rely heavily on the statements of others, even within their own area of expertise."[43] This does not prevent participation nor does it prevent democracy. The fact that the world is complex is no basis for judging democracy impossible or judging citizens inadequate.

Even so, it is possible – in fact, it is necessary – to make expertise safe, or at least more safe, for democracy. This can be done in three ways. First, if experts are to have special authority in our governing process, access to professional careers should be open to all, that is, there should be equal opportunities for higher education. Second, professional training should include education in democratic values. Can we do better to train professionals to consult broadly, to understand the peculiar demands on leadership in a democratic context, to learn to listen, to learn to understand and appreciate cultural differences, to learn humility as well as pride in their work, to learn the limits as well as the capacities of their specialized knowledge? Some professional education works self-consciously to do exactly this, as at the medical schools that require students to read Anne Fadiman's *The Spirit Catches You and You Fall Down*, a remarkable work of reportage that raises troubling questions about the culture of organized medicine in the United States and the arrogance of medical knowledge in relation to the medical beliefs and practices of a distant culture, that of the Hmong.[44] Third, in establishing positions for experts in governing, the full range of institutional and cultural mechanisms for keeping the experts accountable can be employed. These include not only a robust public discussion in which the work of experts can be criticized, but multiple institutional mechanisms to remind experts of the limits of their authority – the dependence of the experts for office or for budget on legislatures or the Congress, the institutional review of their work, carefully written job descriptions, and codes of ethics. "Can authority be democratic?" asks political theorist Mark Warren. He answers that it can, because authority in a democracy, properly constituted, "involves a limited suspension of judgment," not a surrender of judgment, "enabled by a context of democratic challenge and public accountability."[45]

Just as important as making experts safe for democracy, democracy must become safe, or safer, for expertise. It is in the interest of democracy that experts have the support of their professional communities to pursue truth as best they can, that public culture understands and praises nonpartisanship in the exercise of professional judgment, that government provides protection for whistle-blowers who work inside the government, and that in general it becomes at least somewhat more difficult for experts to be intimidated or seduced by the politicians or bureaucrats they work for. It is important that the mainstream news media take it for granted that it is a scandal when Bush administration officials seek to silence government experts or to discount or distort their findings for political purposes. Democracies can and should encourage experts to be expert, can and should protect their autonomy, can and should make good use of expertise in making policy. Radical democrats, with a small "d," do not have to like the authority of experts. They are free to prefer the authority of everyday experience, the authority of the jury, or the authority of the voting booth. But they should still consider that the real world requires specialized knowledge and that the public good will be better secured when experts stand with integrity for the knowledge they claim and not for the elected or appointed barons they serve.

Notes

1 Introduction: facts and democracy

1 Hannah Arendt, *Between Past and Future* (New York: Viking, 1968) p. 231.
2 Ibid., p. 238.
3 Ibid., p. 239.
4 Ibid., p. 261.
5 Walter Lippmann, *Liberty and the News* (Princeton: Princeton University Press, 2007). Originally published in 1920.
6 George Kateb, "The Moral Distinctiveness of Representative Democracy" in Kateb, *The Inner Ocean* (Ithaca, NY: Cornell University Press, 1992) p. 40. This essay originally appeared in *Ethics* 91 (1981).
7 Ibid., p. 41.
8 For an excellent account of news coverage of US detainee abuse in Afghanistan and Iraq, see Eric Umansky, "Failures of Imagination," *Columbia Journalism Review* (September/October, 2006).
9 Arendt, p. 260.

2 Six or seven things news can do for democracy

1 James Carey, "Afterword: The Culture in Question" in Eve Stryker Munson and Catherine A. Warren, eds., *James Carey: A Critical Reader* (Minneapolis: University of Minnesota Press, 1997) p. 332.
2 Robert DeMaria, Jr., *The Life of Samuel Johnson* (Oxford: Blackwell, 1994) pp. 51–6.
3 Michael Schudson, *Discovering the News* (New York: Basic Books, 1978) p. 24.

4   Victor Navasky, *A Matter of Opinion* (New York: Farrar Straus Giroux, 2005) p. 336.

5   Personal communication from Robert A. Kittle, editorial page editor, *San Diego Union-Tribune*, January 31, 2008, informs me that, while the paper did regularly endorse Cunningham, this was in a safe Republican district where neither the Democratic Party nor Republican challengers offered credible opposition. Cunningham was not, Kittle writes, one of the editorial board's "favorites."

6   Charles DuHigg, "Aged, Frail and Denied Care by Their Insurers," *New York Times*, March 26, 2007, A1.

7   Mike Hoyt, "Editorial: Iraq and the Cost of Coverage," *Columbia Journalism Review* (November/December 2007) p. 4.

8   I did not fully trust my memory on this and contacted Roger Wilkins to confirm. He replied, "I think I said something like what you've written and in any event it surely sounds to me like me" (January 2, 2008, personal communication). Wilkins is presently a professor of history at George Mason University.

9   C. Wright Mills, *The Sociological Imagination* (New York: Oxford University Press, 1959).

10 These assertions about the recency of this form are based on work-in-progress analyzing the *New York Times* front page from the 1960s to the present. Initial findings from analyzing a week of front pages every five years from 1967 to 2007 indicates that almost all leads in 1967 were conventional "who-what-when-where" summaries of the event the story focused on. By 2002 and 2007, such leads represented less than half of all leads, replaced primarily by more analytical and interpretive leads that did not always center on an event of the past 24 hours and, to a lesser extent, by "anecdotal leads" that began with an account of an individual's personal trouble and only several paragraphs into the story linked it to a public issue.

11 See Shanto Iyengar and Donald Kinder, *News That Matters* (Chicago: University of Chicago Press, 1987) pp. 34–46.

12 Joseph Raz, *Ethics in the Public Domain* (Oxford: Clarendon Press, 1994) p. 140.

13 Barron Lerner, *When Illness Goes Public: Celebrity Patients and How We Look at Medicine* (Baltimore: Johns Hopkins University Press, 2006).

14 Martin Montgomery, "Broadcast News, the Live 'Two-Way' and the Case of Andrew Gilligan," *Media, Culture and Society* 28 (2006) pp. 233–59.

15 David Ryfe, "News, Culture and Public Life: A Study of 19th-Century American Journalism," *Journalism Studies* 7 (2006) pp. 60–77.

16 See Michael Schudson, "The Concept of Politics in Contemporary U.S. Journalism," *Political Communication* 24 (2007) pp. 131–42.

17 Telling that long story is the aim of Schudson, *Discovering the News*, and it is told again more briefly and with more theoretical self-consciousness in Michael Schudson, "The Objectivity Norm in American Journalism," *Journalism* 2 (August 2001) pp. 149–70.

18 Michael Schudson, *The Good Citizen: A History of American Civic Life* (New York: Free Press, 1998) pp. 144–87.

19 Kent Asp, "Fairness, Informativeness and Scrutiny: The Role of News Media in Democracy," *Nordicom Review*, Jubilee Issue (2007) pp. 31–49 at p. 32.

20 See Enrique Peruzzotti and Catalina Smulovitz, eds., *Enforcing the Rule of Law: Social Accountability in the New Latin American Democracies* (Pittsburgh: University of Pittsburgh Press, 2006).

21 See Jan Schaffer, *Citizen Media: Fad or the Future of News?* (College Park, MD: J-Lab, 2007). This report is available online at www.kcnn.org/research/citizen_media_report.

3 The US model of journalism: exception or exemplar?

1   Benjamin Franklin, *Autobiography* (New York: New American Library, 1961) p. 32.

2   Donald Ritchie, *The Press Gallery* (Cambridge, MA: Harvard University Press, 1991) p. 4.

3   Culves H. Smith, *The Press, Politics, and Patronage* (Athens, GA: University of Georgia Press, 1977) p. 90.

4   Harry J. Carman and Reinhard H. Luthin, *Lincoln and the Patronage* (Gloucester, MA: Peter Smith, 1964) pp. 70–4, 121–8.

5   Alexis de Tocqueville, *Democracy in America* (Garden City, NY: Doubleday, 1969) p. 517.

6   Ibid., p. 519.

7   David Paul Russo, "The Origins of Local News in the U.S. Country Press, 1840s–1870s," *Journalism Monographs* 645 (February 1980) p. 2.

8   Richard Kielbowicz, *News in the Mail* (New York: Greenwood Press, 1989) p. 63.

9   Stuart Blumin, *The Urban Threshold* (Chicago: University of Chicago Press, 1976) pp. 126–49.

10 Daniel Boorstin, *The Americans: The National Experience* (New York: Random House, 1965) p. 141.

11 Sally F. Griffith, *Home Town News: William Allen White and the Emporia Gazette* (New York: Oxford University Press, 1989) p. 14.

12 David Broder, "Political Reporters in Presidential Politics" in Charles Peters and J. Rothchild, eds., *Inside the System* (New York: Praeger, 1973) p. 235.

13 Michael Schudson, *The Good Citizen: A History of American Civic Life* (New York: Free Press, 1998), and Michael McGerr, *The Decline of Popular Politics* (New York: Oxford University Press, 1986).

14 Michael Schudson, *The Power of News* (Cambridge, MA: Harvard University Press, 1995) pp. 72–93.

15 Edwin Emery, Michael Emery, and Nancy Roberts, *The Press and America* (Englewood Cliffs, NJ: Prentice-Hall, 1996) p. 181.

16 Elliot King, "Ungagged Partisanship: The Political Values of the Public Press, 1835–1920," 1992, Ph.D. diss., University of California, San Diego, pp. 396–8, 467–8.

17 Michael Schudson, "The Objectivity Norm in American Journalism," *Journalism* 2 (2001) pp. 149–70.

18 Michael Schudson, *Discovering the News* (New York: Basic Books, 1978) p. 143.

19 John Dewey, *Individualism Old and New* (New York: Minton, Balch, 1930) p. 43.

20 Walter Lippmann, *Liberty and the News* (Princeton: Princeton University Press, 2007) (originally published in 1920) pp. 67, 82.

21 Jean Chalaby, "Journalism as an Anglo-American Invention: A Comparison of the Development of French and Anglo-American Journalism, 1830s–1920s," *European Journal of Communication* 11 (1996) pp. 303–26.

22 Daniel Hallin, *We Keep America on Top of the World* (New York: Routledge, 1994) pp. 170–80.

23 Herbert J. Gans, *Deciding What's News* (New York: Pantheon Books, 1979) pp. 39–55.

24 *New York Times* v. *Sullivan* 376 US 270.

25 Owen Fiss, "The Censorship of Television" in Lee Bollinger and Geoffrey Stone, eds., *Eternally Vigilant* (Chicago: University of Chicago Press, 2002) pp. 257–83.

26 Owen Fiss, *Liberalism Divided* (Boulder, CO: Westview Press, 1996) p. 35.

27 F. Plasser, "Parties' Diminishing Relevance for Campaign Professionals," *Harvard International Journal of Press/Politics* 6 (2001) p. 49.

28 Nancy Rosenblum, "Navigating Pluralism: The Democracy of Everyday Life (and Where It Is Learned)" in Stephen Elkin and Karol Soltan, eds., *Citizen Competence and Democratic Institutions* (University Park, PA: Pennsylvania State University Press, 1999) pp. 72–3, 78–9.

4 The invention of the American newspaper as popular art, 1890–1930

1 Peter Schjeldahl, "Fanfares for the Common Man," *New Yorker*, November 22, 1999, pp. 190–3, 196 at p. 193.

2 Richard Terdiman, *Discourse/Counter-Discourse* (Ithaca: Cornell University Press, 1985) p. 125.

3 Ibid., p. 127.

4 *San Diego Union*, June 19, 1891, 7.

5 Bernard Berelson, "What Missing the Newspaper Means" in Paul Lazarsfeld and Frank Stanton eds., *Communications Research 1948–1949* (New York: Harper and Brothers, 1949) pp. 36–47.

6 Michael McGerr, *The Decline of Popular Politics: The American North, 1865–1928* (New York: Oxford University Press, 1986).

7 Ibid., p. 120.

8   See Michael Schudson, *Discovering the News* (New York: Basic Books, 1978) pp. 121–59.
9   Oliver Gramling, *AP: The Story of News* (New York: Farrar and Rinehart, 1940) p. 314.
10 Paul Pratte, *Gods Within the Machine: A History of the American Society of Newspaper Editors, 1923–1993* (Westport, CT: Praeger, 1995) p. 206.
11 James E. Cebula, *James M. Cox: Journalist and Politician* (New York: Garland Publishing, 1985) p. 21.
12 Meyer Berger, *The Story of the New York Times 1851–1951* (New York: Simon & Schuster, 1951) p. 424.
13 Martin Wattenberg, *The Decline of American Political Parties 1952–1994* (Cambridge, MA: Harvard University Press, 1996) p. 151. Data from *Editor and Publisher* surveys. Close to 70 percent endorsed in 1960, nearer to 80 percent in the next several elections, and then the figure was down to 62 percent in 1980, 67 percent in 1984, and 45 percent in 1988.
14 "The Press and the Public," special section of *New Republic* 90 (March 17, 1937) p. 185. See, generally, Schudson, *Discovering the News*, pp. 150–1, and Graham J. White, *FDR and the Press* (Chicago: University of Chicago Press, 1979) pp. 27–32.
15 For some instances of newspapers rejecting columns, see White, *FDR and the Press*, pp. 94–5.
16 Betty Houchin Winfield, *FDR and the News Media* (New York: Columbia University Press, 1994) pp. 64, 82.
17 This is the account provided in Ronald Steel, *Walter Lippmann and the American Century* (Boston: Atlantic Monthly Press, 1980) pp. 418–19. James Reston, in his memoir, *Deadline* (New York: Random House, 1991) pp. 156–61, offers a more circumspect account in which Walter Lippmann's name does not appear. For a fuller account of this incident and other examples of implicit or explicit partisanship in newspapers in the 1930s, 1940s, 1950s, and 1960s, see Michael Schudson, "Persistence of Vision" in Carl Kaestle and Janice Radway, eds., *The History of the Book in America*, vol. IV: *The Mainstream Partisan Press* (Chapel Hill: University of North Carolina Press, forthcoming).

5   Why democracies need an unlovable press

1   Alexis de Tocqueville, *Democracy in America*, ed. J. P. Myer (Garden City, NY: Doubleday, 1969) p. 180.
2   W. Lance Bennett, "Toward a Theory of Press–State Relations in the United States," *Journal of Communication* 40 (Spring, 1990) pp. 103–125 at 106, 125.
3   Herbert Gans, *Democracy and the News* (New York: Oxford University Press, 2003). Gans and Bennett, like many other contemporary theorists, both

presume not only that the press at its best should report the doings of government but that it should do so in ways that encourage and provide for the participation of ordinary citizens, informing them in advance of governmental decisions so that they can make their voices heard. This is by no means an undisputed assumption. As John Zaller has argued, the job of the press in a mass democracy may be to help people evaluate leaders, not policies. The press should try to make it possible for the public to evaluate leaders after they have acted, not policies before they have been put in place. See John Zaller, "Elite Leadership of Mass Opinion: New Evidence from the Gulf War" in W. Lance Bennett and David Paletz, eds., *Taken By Storm: The Media, Public Opinion, and U.S. Foreign Policy in the Gulf War* (Chicago: University of Chicago Press, 1994) pp. 201–2.

4   See Herbert J. Gans, *Deciding What's News* (New York: Pantheon Books, 1979).

5   Janet Steele, "Experts and the Operational Bias of Television News: The Case of the Persian Gulf War," *Journalism and Mass Communication Quarterly* 72 (1995) pp. 799–812.

6   Daniel Hallin, Robert Manoff, and Judy Weddle, "Sourcing Patterns of National Security Reporters," *Journalism and Mass Communication Quarterly* 70 (1993) pp. 753–66.

7   Thomas Ferenczi, "The Media and Democracy," *CSD Bulletin* 8/1 (London: Centre for the Study of Democracy, Winter 2000–1) pp. 1–2.

8   The most notable exceptions are Harvey Molotch and Marilyn Lester, "Accidents, Scandals, and Routines: Resources for Insurgent Methodology," *Insurgent Sociologist* 3 (1973) pp. 1–11, and Regina Lawrence, *The Politics of Force* (Berkeley: University of California Press, 2000). And I would like to add, however belatedly, me – see *The Sociology of News* (New York: W. W. Norton, 2003) pp. 1–8, from which I borrow here.

9   Scholars have not ignored the question of journalistic autonomy. They have provided important explanations for this autonomy. Daniel Hallin sees autonomy provided structurally by divisions among elites. Daniel C. Hallin, *"The Uncensored War": The Media and Vietnam* (New York: Oxford University Press, 1956). You can see it also in laws that make it tough to sue for libel. These explanations direct attention to structural opportunities for aggressive reporting, but they do not provide journalists with a motive to pursue, challenge, and critique.

10   Edward Jay Epstein, *News From Nowhere* (New York: Random House, 1973) p. 31, found that journalists had at least 24 hours' notice for more than 90 percent of stories on the NBC evening news. "Wholly unpredictable events" made up less than 2 percent of stories.

11   Lawrence, p. 188.

12   The story stayed in the news as the conflict widened – see Randal Archibold, "Indian Point Is Safe, N.R.C. Official Says," *New York Times*, February 22, 2003, A18, and the Op-Ed column by Herschel Specter, "Nuclear Risk and Reality," *New York Times*, May 20, 2003, A31.

13   This is not to mention background stories that are exclusively focused on stagecraft. See, for instance, Elisabeth Bumiller, "Keepers of Bush Image Lift Stagecraft to New Heights," *New York Times*, May 16, 2003, 1.

14   *New York Times*, September 30, 2003, A4.

15   Heather E. Gorgura, "Lott Gets a Blogging: Did the Amateur Journalists of the Blogosphere Bring Down Trent Lott?" March 2003, unpublished paper, University of Washington. This student paper is extremely thoughtful and well documented.

16   Or so I said when this chapter was originally published in 2005. In 2008, a number of political blogs and other blogs have attracted enough advertising to make money.

17   See Mickey Kaus, "Kausfiles," September 22, 2003, at http://slate.msn.com and www.laobserved.com, September 23, 2003 and September 24, 2003.

18   September 20, 2003 e-mail from Jill Zuckman.

6   The concept of politics in contemporary US journalism

1   Herbert J. Gans, *Deciding What's News* (New York: Pantheon, 1979) p. 68.

2   Ibid., p. 43.

3   Ibid.

4   Ibid.

5   Ibid., p. 44.

6   Ibid.

7   Ibid., pp. 51–2.

8   Ibid. p. 45.

9   Lizette Alvarez, "Senate Passes Bill for Annual Tests in Public Schools," *New York Times*, June 15, 2001, A1.

10   D. Espo, "Sweeping Education Reform Bill Wins OK," *San Diego Union-Tribune*, June 15, 2001, A1.

11   Michael McGerr, *The Decline of Popular Politics* (New York: Oxford University Press, 1986); Michael Schudson, *The Power of News* (Cambridge, MA: Harvard University Press, 1995); Michael Schudson, *The Good Citizen: A History of American Civic Life* (New York: Free Press, 1998).

12   Andrew Sullivan, "TRB: After Party," *New Republic*, June 11, 2001, 8.

13   "News in Brief," *Onion*, August 3–9, 2006, 2.

14   Edmund Morris, *The Rise of Theodore Roosevelt* (New York: Ballantine, 1979) p. 398.

15   Paul Van Riper, *History of the United States Civil Service* (Evanston, IL: Row, Peterson, 1958) p. 81.

16   Tim Egan, "For Thirsty Farmers, Old Friends at Interior Dept," *New York Times*, March 3, 2006, A1.

17   Gans, p. 44.

18   The classic study of how the media marginalize or deride non-electoral protest is Todd Gitlin, *The Whole World Is Watching* (Berkeley: University of California Press, 1980).

19 Gans, p. 44.
20 See www.firstamendmentcenter.org/news.aspx?id=16593.
21 Gans, p. 45.
22 Stephen Ansolabehere, E. Snowberg, and J. Snyder, "Unrepresentative Information: The Case of Newspaper Reporting on Campaign Finance," *Public Opinion Quarterly* 69 (Summer) pp. 213–31.
23 Angela Lau, "'Ban the Ban' Got Funds From Alcohol Sellers," *San Diego Union-Tribune*, August 2, 2001, B1.
24 Claire Vannette, "If This Makes You Dizzy, It's Not the Booze," 2001, paper for undergraduate class, University of California, San Diego.
25 Gans, p. 44.
26 Thomas Patterson, "Doing Well and Doing Good: How Soft News and Critical Journalism Are Shrinking the News Audience and Weakening Democracy – And What News Outlets Can Do About It," Cambridge, MA: Joan Shorenstein Center on Press, Politics, and Public Policy, Kennedy School of Government, Harvard University, 2000, p. 14.
27 David E. Sanger, "Bush Honors D-Day Troops at Dedication of Memorial," *New York Times*, June 7, 2001, A28.
28 David E. Sanger, "Dr. King Is Hailed by Bush in Event at the White House," *New York Times*, January 22, 2002, A16.
29 Richard L. Berke, "In Personal Anecdote, Some See New Distance Where Others See New Strategy," *New York Times*, January 24, 2002, C6.
30 Schudson, *The Good Citizen*.
31 William Haltom and Michael McCann, *Distorting the Law: Politics, Media, and the Litigation Crisis* (Chicago: University of Chicago Press, 2004).
32 Richard Abel, "The Real Tort Crisis – Too Few Claims," *Ohio State Law Journal* 48 (1987) pp. 443–67 at p. 467.
33 N. R. Kleinfield, "Streets of No Escape," *New York Times*, January 9, 2006, A1; January 10, 2006, A1; January 11, 2006, A1; and January 12, 2006, A1. A. Elliott, "An Imam in America," *New York Times*, March 5, 2006, A1; March 6, 2006, A1; and March 7, 2006, A1. A. Lehren and J. Leland, "Parental Notice Has Scant Effect in Teen Abortion," *New York Times*, March 6, 2006, A1. Jason DeParle, "Katrina's Tide Carries Many to Hopeful Shores," *New York Times*, April 23, 2006, A1.

7 What's unusual about covering politics as usual

1 Bill Carter and Felicity Barringer, "In Patriotic Time, Dissent is Muted," *New York Times*, September 28, 2001, A1.
2 Robin Toner, "Bush Law-Enforcement Plan Troubles Both Right and Left," *New York Times*, September 28, 2001, A1.
3 Evelyn Nieves, "Recalling Internment and Saying 'Never Again,'" *New York Times*, September 28, 2001, A14.

4   Melody Peterson, "Reports of Scams Preying on Donors Are on Rise," *New York Times*, September 28, 2001, A18.

5   Bruce Lambert, "8,000 Residents, Still Displaced, Grow Frustrated And Then Angry," *New York Times*, September 28, 2001, A25.

6   Jennifer Steinhauer, "Giuliani Takes Charge, and City Sees Him as the Essential Man," *New York Times*, September 14, 2001, A2.

7   John Tierney, "Most Heroes Would Go, But Giuliani Isn't Most," *New York Times*, September 28, 2001, A26.

8   "The Mayor's Dangerous Idea" (editorial), *New York Times*, September 28, 2001, A30.

9   Dennis Overbye, "Engineers Tackle Havoc Underground," *New York Times*, September 18, 2001, D1.

10 Kenneth Chang, "Defending Skyscrapers Against Terror," *New York Times*, September 18, 2001, D1.

11 Natalie Angier, "Of Altruism, Heroism and Evolution's Gifts," *New York Times*, September 18, 2001, D1.

12 James Glanz and Andrew C. Revkin, "Haunting Question: Did the Ban on Asbestos Lead to Loss of Life?" *New York Times*, September 18, 2001, D2.

13 Andrew C. Revkin, "Dust Is a Problem, but the Risk Seems Small," *New York Times*, September 18, 2001, D2.

14 William J. Broad, "Making Planes Safer By Making Fuels Safer," *New York Times*, September 18, 2001, D3.

15 Sandeep Jauhar, "They Had Everything They Needed, Except Survivors to Treat," *New York Times*, September 18, 2001, D3; Abigail Zuger, "They Had Everything They Needed, Except Survivors to Treat," *New York Times*, September 18, 2001, D3.

16 Lawrence K. Altman, "Donors Flood Blood Banks, but a Steady Stream Is What's Needed," *New York Times*, September 18, 2001, D4.

17 Jane E. Brody, "During Traumatic Times, Small Acts Can Bring a Measure of Comfort," *New York Times*, September 18, 2001, D4.

18 James W. Carey, "Why and How? The Dark Continent of American Journalism" in Robert Manoff and Michael Schudson, eds., *Reading the News* (New York: Pantheon, 1986) pp. 146–96, at pp. 151–2.

19 "The Faces Emerge" (editorial), *New York Times*, September 16, 2001, Sect. 4, 10.

20 Jane Gross, "A Muted Christmas, Corporate Obligations, the Anthrax Mystery," *New York Times*, December 26, 2001, B1.

21 Ellen Goodman, "Post Sept. 11 Dilemmas for Journalists," *San Diego Union-Tribune*, December 7, 2001, B12.

22 Tom Brokaw, "Two Dates Which Will Live in Infamy," *San Diego Union-Tribune*, December 7, 2001, B13.

23 Daniel C. Hallin, *"The Uncensored War": The Media and Vietnam* (New York: Oxford University Press, 1986) p. 116.

24 Ibid., p. 117.

25 Ibid.

26 Harold Evans, "Warning Given . . . Story Missed," *Columbia Journalism Review* (November/December, 2001) pp. 12–14.
27 James Fallows, "The *New York Times*: A Civic Nomination," *Civic Catalyst* (Winter 2002) p. 17. Reprinted from *Slate*, December 3, 2001.
28 Nick Spangler, "Witness," *Columbia Journalism Review* (November/December 2001) pp. 6–9.
29 Katherine E. Finkelstein, "40 Hours in Hell," *American Journalism Review* 23 (November 2001) pp. 28–33.
30 Orville Schell, "The Media Clarified," *North Gate News* (newsletter of the Graduate School of Journalism University of California, Berkeley) 28/8 (Fall 2001) p. 9.
31 Ivan Carvalho, "Alumnus LeDuff Chronicles Lives Lost," *North Gate News* (newsletter of the Graduate School of Journalism, University of California, Berkeley) 28/8 (Fall 2001) p. 3.
32 Yoram Peri, "The Rabin Myth and the Press: Reconstruction of the Israeli Collective Identity," *European Journal of Communication* 12 (1997) pp. 435–58.
33 Slavenka Drakulic, *Café Europa: Life After Communism* (New York: W. W. Norton, 1996) p. 2.
34 Hallin, p. 127.
35 Linda Greenhouse, "The Clamor of a Free People," *New York Times*, September 16, 2001, Sect. 4, 1.
36 Joseph N. Cappella and Kathleen Hall Jamieson, *Spiral of Cynicism* (New York: Oxford University Press, 1997); Thomas E. Patterson, *Out of Order* (New York: Alfred A. Knopf, 1993).
37 Michael Schudson, "Is Journalism Hopelessly Cynical?" in Sam Kernell and Steven S. Smith, eds., *Principles and Practices of American Politics* (Washington, DC: CQ Press, 2000) pp. 742–51.

8 The anarchy of events and the anxiety of story telling

1 There is a large literature on the sociology of news production. I have summarized it in Michael Schudson, *The Sociology of News* (New York: W. W. Norton, 2003), and provided a review of the literature in James Curran and Michael Gurevitch, eds., *Mass Media and Society*, 4th edn. (London: Hodder Arnold, 2005) pp. 173–97.
2 Elisabeth Anker, "Villains, Victims, and Heroes: Melodrama, Media, and September 11," *Journal of Communication* 55 (2005) pp. 22–37, at p. 36.
3 James Ettema, "Crafting Cultural Resonance: Imaginative Power in Everyday Journalism," *Journalism: Theory, Practice, Criticism* 6 (May 2005) pp. 131–52.
4 Walter R. Mears, "A Reporter's Look at the 2004 Campaign," *Journalism Studies* 6 (2005) p. 231.

9 Why conversation is not the soul of democracy

1 Jürgen Habermas, "The Public Sphere," *New German Critique* 1 (1974) p. 49.
2 The definition is adapted from A. D. Lindsay in Stephen Holmes, *Passions and Constraint* (Chicago: University of Chicago Press, 1995) p. 71.
3 John Dewey, *The Public and Its Problems* (New York: Henry Holt, 1927) p. 208.
4 David Simpson, *The Academic Postmodern and the Role of Literature* (Chicago: University of Chicago Press, 1995) p. 47, and David Simpson, "The Cult of 'Conversation'", *Raritan* 16 (Spring 1997) pp. 75–85.
5 James W. Carey, "The Press, Public Opinion, and Public Discourse" in Theodore L. Glasser and Charles T. Salmon, eds., *Public Opinion and the Communication of Consent* (New York: Guilford Press, 1995) pp. 373–402.
6 Peter Burke, *The Art of Conversation* (Cambridge: Polity Press, 1995) p. 106, citing a manual of 1672 by Charles Sorel.
7 Ibid., p. 92.
8 Michael Oakeshott, "The Voice of Poetry in the Conversation of Mankind" in Michael Oakeshott, *Rationalism in Politics* (New York: Basic Books, 1962) p. 198.
   Gabriel Tarde, too, stresses that conversation is non-utilitarian. He defines it as "any dialogue without direct and immediate utility, in which one talks primarily to talk, for pleasure, as a game, out of politeness." See Gabriel Tarde, "Opinion and Conversation" in Gabriel Tarde, *On Communication and Social Influence* ed. Terry N. Clark (Chicago: University of Chicago Press, 1969) p. 304.
9 Oakeshott, p. 199.
10 Dewey, p. 206.
11 Ibid., p. 219. Oakeshott presumably had no particular use for experts – there is no notion that "expertise" is required for participating in conversation; cultivation is, and that is quite different. But if Oakeshott is no defender of expertise, Dewey is quite directly a critic. "It is impossible," he writes, "for high-brows to secure a monopoly of such knowledge as must be used for the regulation of common affairs. In the degree in which they become a specialized class, they are shut off from knowledge of the needs which they are supposed to serve."
12 See James W. Carey, *Communication As Culture* (Boston: Unwin Hyman, 1989) pp. 69–88.
13 William Galston, *Liberal Purposes* (Cambridge: Cambridge University Press, 1991) p. 227.
14 Paul Grice, "Logic and Conversation" (1975) in Paul Grice, *Studies in the Way of Words* (Cambridge, MA: Harvard University Press, 1989) p. 26.
15 Jane Mansbridge, *Beyond Adversary Democracy* (New York: Basic Books, 1980) pp. 60–4, 106.

16 See Michael Schudson, "Embarrassment and Erving Goffman's Idea of Human Nature," *Theory and Society* 13 (1984) pp. 633–48.

17 I have developed this distinction from suggestions made to me by Elihu Katz.

18 Stephen Macedo, *Liberal Virtues* (Oxford: Clarendon Press, 1990) p. 103.

19 Ibid., p. 40.

20 Bruce Ackerman, "Why Dialogue?" *Journal of Philosophy* 86 (1989) pp. 5–22 at p. 6.

21 Erving Goffman, *Forms of Talk* (Philadelphia: University of Pennsylvania Press, 1981) pp. 70–1.

22 Harold Pinter, *A Slight Ache* in *Three Plays* (New York: Grove, 1962). I used this quotation some years ago in an earlier and very different effort to understand the role of conversation in thinking about the mass media and, secondarily in that effort, democracy. See Michael Schudson, "The Ideal of Conversation in the Study of Mass Media," *Communication Research* 5 (1978) pp. 320–9.

23 Tarde, p. 304.

24 Ibid., p. 312.

25 Ibid., pp. 317–18.

26 Dewey, p. 218.

27 George Kateb, *The Inner Ocean* (Ithaca, NY: Cornell University Press, 1992) p. 40.

28 Political talk in public settings may even be derided, as it was at the end of the nineteenth century for taking place in the boisterous territory of the street rather than the civil setting of the home. A New Jersey newspaper praised the "silent, thinking men . . . who go quietly day after day about their business of earning a livelihood and who at night are found in their homes instead of talking politics on street corners." *Trenton True American*, November 6, 1911, cited in John Reynolds, *Testing Democracy* (Chapel Hill: University of North Carolina Press, 1988) p. 120.

29 Stephen Holmes, *Passions and Constraint* (Chicago: University of Chicago Press, 1995) pp. s202–35.

10 The trouble with experts – and why democracies need them

1 James G. March and Johan P. Olsen, *Democratic Governance* (New York: Free Press, 1995) p. 178.

2 The idea of the political observatory is a key element in Lippmann's proposals for making democracy work in *Public Opinion*, but the colorful phrase itself does not appear there but in his book *Liberty and the News* (New York: Harcourt, Brace and Hone, 1920) p. 5.

3 John Dewey, *The Public and Its Problems* (New York: Henry Holt, 1927) p. 139.

4 Ibid., pp. 207–8.

5   "The quack, defined functionally and not in evaluative terms, is the man who continues through time to please his customers but not his colleagues." This appeared originally in a 1951 article, "Mistakes at Work," reprinted in Everett C. Hughes, *The Sociological Eye: Selected Papers* (Chicago: Aldine, 1971) p. 322.

6   Thomas S. Kuhn, *The Structure of Scientific Revolutions* (Chicago: University of Chicago Press, 1962) p. 151.

7   On law, see Jerold Auerbach, *Unequal Justice* (New York: Oxford University Press, 1976); on medicine, see Ivan Illich, *Medical Nemesis* (New York: Pantheon, 1976), and Barbara Ehrenreich and Deirdre English, *Complaints and Disorders: The Sexual Politics of Sickness* (Old Westbury, NY: Feminist Press, 1973); on psychiatry, see R. D. Laing, *The Divided Self* (New York: Pantheon, 1969), Thomas Szasz, *The Myth of Mental Illness* (New York: Harper and Row, 1961), Thomas Szasz, *Law, Liberty, and Psychiatry* (New York: Macmillan, 1963), and Thomas Szasz, *The Manufacture of Madness* (New York: Harper and Row, 1970); on sociology, see Robert Friedrichs, *A Sociology of Sociology* (New York: Free Press, 1970); on professionals generally, see Burton Bledstein, *The Culture of Professionalism* (New York: W. W. Norton, 1976) – and this is just a sample.

8   Michel Foucault, *Power/Knowledge: Selected Interviews and Other Writings 1972–1977*, ed. Colin Gordon (New York: Pantheon, 1980) p. 118.

9   Ibid., p. 131.

10 Donna Haraway, "Situated Knowledges: The Science Question in Feminism and the Privilege of the Partial Perspective," *Feminist Studies* 14 (1988) pp. 575–99.

11 Stephen P. Turner, *Liberal Democracy 3.0* (London: SAGE, 2003) pp. 19–23.

12 Ian Shapiro, "Three Ways to Be a Democrat," *Political Theory* 22 (1994) pp. 124–51, p. 140. Shapiro borrows from himself here, making the argument that he made in "Principled Criticism and the Democratic Ethos" in Ian Shapiro, *Political Criticism* (Berkeley: University of California Press, 1990) pp. 283–5.

13 Ibid., p. 141.

14 Ibid.

15 Ibid., pp. 141–2.

16 Jeffrey Abramson, *We, the Jury* (New York: Basic Books, 1994) pp. 116–17.

17 See Stephan Landsman, "The Civil Jury in America," *Law and Contemporary Problems* 62 (1999) p. 295; William V. Luneburg and Mark A. Nordenberg, "Specially Qualified Juries and Expert Nonjury Tribunals: Alternatives for Coping with the Complexities of Modern Civil Litigation," *Virginia Law Review* 67 (1981) pp. 887–1007; and Stephen F. Sherry, "Don't Let Amateurs Decide," *IP Law and Business* (December, 2004), available at www.iplawandbusiness.com. There have been debates about the role of juries in complex cases in both Britain and New Zealand. See Neil Cameron, Susan

Potter, and Warren Young, "The New Zealand Jury," *Law and Contemporary Problems* 62 (1999) pp. 117–18. On the use of special masters in complex litigation, see Georgene Vairo, "Why Me? The Role of Private Trustees in Complex Claims Resolution," *Stanford Law Review* 57 (2005) pp. 1391–428.

18 See Andrew J. Wistrich, Chris Guthrie, and Jeffrey J. Rachlinski, "Can Judges Ignore Inadmissible Information? The Difficulty of Deliberately Disregarding," *University of Pennsylvania Law Review* 153 (2005) pp. 1251–345.

19 Sally Lloyd-Bostock and Cheryl Thomas, "Decline of the 'Little Parliament': Juries and Jury Reform in England and Wales," *Law and Contemporary Problems* 62 (1999) pp. 13, 15.

20 For example, close to two-thirds of trials in felony cases are jury trials, even though only a small percentage of felony cases go to trial at all. See Nancy Jean King, "The American Criminal Jury," *Law and Contemporary Problems* 62 (1999) p. 59.

21 Robert Jay Lifton, *The Nazi Doctors: Medical Killing and the Psychology of Genocide* (New York: Basic Books, 1986).

22 Robert Jay Lifton, "Doctors and Torture," *New England Journal of Medicine* 352 (July 29, 2004) pp. 415–16.

23 Steven H. Miles, "Abu Ghraib: Its Legacy for Military Medicine," *Lancet* 364 (August 21, 2004) pp. 725–9.

24 David Halberstam, *The Best and the Brightest* (New York: Random House, 1972). On McNamara, see pp. 257–9; on Rusk, 266–7; on Stilwell, 280. This is just a sampling. The book's argument consistently supports experts and attacks the proud but ignorant social elite running foreign policy in Vietnam. Halberstam quotes John Kenneth Galbraith (p. 60) saying that "their expertise was nothing . . . mostly a product of social background and a certain kind of education." To Galbraith, the likes of McGeorge Bundy and others who learned their foreign policy through the elite Council on Foreign Relations knew little of the United States and "had not traveled around the world" and so knew nothing of other nations, either.

25 Thomas Haskell, *Objectivity Is Not Neutrality: Explanatory Schemes in History* (Baltimore: Johns Hopkins University Press, 1998) p. 177.

26 Ibid., p. 178.

27 Chris Mooney, *The Republican War on Science* (New York: Basic Books, 2005).

28 Steven Epstein, "The New Attack on Sexuality Research: Morality and the Politics of Knowledge Production," *Sexual Research and Social Policy* 3 (March 2006) p. 2.

29 Andrew C. Revkin, "Bush Aide Softened Greenhouse Gas Links to Global Warming," *New York Times*, June 8, 2005.

30 Andrew C. Revkin, "Climate Expert Says NASA Tried to Silence Him," *New York Times*, January 29, 2006, available at www.nytimes.com/2006/01/29/science/earth/29climate.html. See also Juliet Eilperin, "Climate Researchers Feeling Heat From White House," *Washington Post*, April 6, 2006, A27.

31 Kevin Phillips, *American Theocracy* (New York: Viking, 2006).

32 Edmund L. Andrews, "As Congressional Budget Chief, Former Bush Economic Aide Isn't Keeping to Script," *New York Times*, August 23, 2004, A12.

33 Steven Epstein, *Impure Science: AIDS, Activism, and the Politics of Knowledge* (Berkeley: University of California Press, 1996).

34 Epstein, "New Attack on Sexuality Research," p. 8.

35 Ian Shapiro, *The State of Democratic Theory* (Princeton: Princeton University Press, 2003) p. 58.

36 Bernard Manin, *The Principles of Representative Government* (Cambridge: Cambridge University Press, 1997). Manin shows that Harrington, Montesquieu, and Rousseau among others took it for granted that selection by lot favored democracy, while elections favored oligarchic or aristocratic rule. The shift to treating election as the essential institution of democracy came in the eighteenth century with a new conception of citizenship – "citizens were now viewed primarily as the source of political legitimacy, rather than as persons who might desire to hold office themselves" (p. 92). When the notion of democracy as a government founded in popular consent replaced a notion of democracy as one in which all citizens would have equal opportunity to govern, then the centrality of elections followed.

37 Quoted in Alan Rosenthal, Burdett Loomis, John Hibbing, and Karl Kurtz, *Republic on Trial: The Case for Representative Democracy* (Washington, DC: CQ Press, 2003) p. 105.

38 Ibid., p. 106.

39 John W. Kingdon, *Congressmen's Voting Decisions* (New York: Harper & Row, 1973) p. 70.

40 C. Lawrence Evans, "How Senators Decide: An Exploration" in Bruce I. Oppenheimer, ed., *U.S. Senate Exceptionalism* (Columbus: Ohio State University Press, 2002) pp. 262–82 at 268–9.

41 Haskell, p. 215.

42 Ibid.

43 Robert Dahl, "The Problem of Civic Competence" in Robert Dahl, *Toward Democracy: A Journey* vol. 1 (Berkeley: Institute of Governmental Studies, 1997) pp. 211–28, at p. 222. (Originally in *Journal of Democracy* 3 (1992) pp. 45–59.)

44 Anne Fadiman, *The Spirit Catches You and You Fall Down* (New York: Farrar Straus Giroux, 1997).

45 Mark E. Warren, "Deliberative Democracy and Authority," *American Political Science Review* 90 (1996) p. 47. Warren's essay is a particularly rich exploration of the problem of authority in a democracy. It is centrally concerned with the apparent contradiction between expertise and democracy. Warren believes, as I do, that there is in the end no contradiction but a need to think through how democratic forms of authority should be constituted.

Index